HARD AS NAILS

HARD AS NAILS

THE GRAHAM ROBERTS STORY

Graham Roberts

with Colin Duncan

BLACK & WHITE PUBLISHING

First published 2008
This edition published 2009
by Black & White Publishing Ltd
29 Ocean Drive, Edinburgh EH6 6JL

1 3 5 7 9 10 8 6 4 2   09 10 11 12 13

ISBN: 978 1 84502 258 7

A CIP catalogue record for this book is available
from the British Library.

Typeset by Ellipsis Books Limited, Glasgow
Printed and bound by Cox & Wyman, Reading

CONTENTS

To my children Hollie, Sasha, Luke and Ella,
and my grandson Joshua

FOREWORD
BY STEVE PERRYMAN

Tottenham Hotspur have spent hundreds of millions in transfer fees over the years, but when it comes to value for money nothing comes remotely close to matching the £30,000 Keith Burkinshaw shelled out to bring Graham Roberts from Weymouth. At a time when £1 million moves were all the rage, Robbo's switch from non-league to the top flight of English football must rank as the bargain of the century.

It immediately became evident that Robbo was something special, slotting effortlessly into a team packed with the finest English talent and two Argentina World Cup winners. A lot of players would have found that sort of arena intimidating. Robbo's incredible self-belief and desire to succeed ensured he didn't look out of place. Even in the exalted company of Glenn Hoddle, Ricky Villa and Ossie Ardiles, the new boy managed to stand out in his own inimitable way.

It was no coincidence that Tottenham enjoyed one of the most successful periods in the club's history at the start of the eighties shortly after Robbo arrived at the club. The supporters always remember him as a hard man and while his swashbuckling style was a key part of his make-up, it shouldn't be forgotten that Robbo could play a bit.

However, his biggest attribute was his spirit and there were so many times when he bailed Tottenham out of trouble with his never-say-die approach. The competitive element in his game was stronger than anybody else I ever played with and not once did he shirk out of a tackle regardless of how badly the odds were stacked against him.

For me, the one game that defined Robbo above all others was the second leg of the 1984 UEFA Cup Final with Anderlecht at White Hart Lane. I was suspended after being booked in the first match when we drew 1-1 and Robbo took over as skipper for the return.

Talk about leading by example. Almost single-handedly he carried the entire team through the match, equalising after the Belgians had taken an early lead and then scoring a crucial spot-kick in the nerve-shredding penalty shoot-out.

It was one of the greatest performances I ever had the pleasure to witness and while I was gutted at not being on the pitch it was fitting that Robbo got to collect the trophy in front of his adoring supporters.

FOREWORD
BY CHRIS WOODS

When the going gets tough, the tough get going. That motto perfectly summed up Graham Roberts during a distinguished career for Spurs, Rangers, Chelsea and England.

I had the privilege of playing behind Robbo for a couple of seasons at Ibrox and we have remained firm friends ever since. A terrific player and an intelligent defender, his biggest quality was undoubtedly his desire to succeed. I was fortunate to play alongside some terrific players during my own career, but nobody had a bigger heart than Robbo.

At Rangers he found himself in a dressing room full of winners and he flourished alongside fiercely competitive team-mates like Terry Butcher, Ally McCoist and Richard Gough. Ibrox was a home from home for him and his never-say-die approach quickly endeared him to the Rangers support.

Robbo only spent eighteen months in Glasgow, yet twenty years later he is still fondly remembered by the fans. That speaks volumes for the impact he made during his short stint in Scottish football.

1

FOURTH TIME LUCKY

David and Victoria Beckham might think they started a trend by naming children after the place where they were conceived, but Reg and Maisie Roberts were miles ahead of the game. Forty years before Brooklyn Beckham was christened after the New York borough where his parents enjoyed a romantic break, I was named after a street in Southampton! It doesn't quite have the same ring to it, but Graham Roberts was born in Graham Road, Southampton on the 3rd of July 1959.

One of six children I was brought up on a less-than-salubrious, sprawling council estate where only the tough and hard-working prospered. Life was difficult for me, Malcolm, Stephen, Shaun, Tina and Sharon, but we all shared a love of football when we were growing up and that provided us with a focus. It also kept us out of trouble as most of the kids I grew up with in the Woolston area of Southampton sooner or later found themselves on the wrong side of the law.

The family passion for football came from both of my parents, although mainly from Mum. She was a fanatic and, believe it or not, she was my manager for the first ten years of my career. Dad was her assistant. I started off at Under 7

1

level and I played every weekend right up until I left school and signed for Bournemouth as an apprentice.

Wildern Sky Blues was the name of our boys' club team and we won everything in the Hampshire area. It was virtually the same group of lads for the best part of a decade and Mum produced some terrific players. Guys like Steve Moran and Graham Baker both went on to play for Southampton and she was responsible for nurturing their talent. I've lost count of all the different bosses I've worked under throughout my career and while it's difficult to remember some of them there's no way I could possibly forget my first. Mum was a formidable woman in her day and while she wouldn't thank me for the comparison, she was straight out of the Graeme Souness school of management.

There weren't too many people who crossed her although underneath that tough exterior, which was really just a front on match days, she had a heart of gold. Still, I always found it best not to tangle with her when we had a game. She was always on edge because she was so engrossed in her football. Unfortunately my older brother Malcolm made the mistake of getting on the wrong side of her one weekend and ended up paying a heavy price.

One Saturday the referee failed to turn up and as Malcolm was an official himself, he agreed to do Mum a favour by taking charge of our game. Both myself and Stephen were in the side although only one of us would see out the ninety minutes as Malcolm red-carded my little brother for swearing. While we still won the game comfortably, Mum was absolutely seething and told Malcolm not to bother coming home that night. He thought she was joking, but when he arrived back at the house later that night his bags were packed. It was a week before Mum calmed down and allowed him back. Incredible, yet that's how much football meant to her.

Another example of her no-nonsense approach came a few years later when we were playing in the semi-final of the Hampshire Cup. The Hampshire Cup was a Sunday League tournament comprising mostly pub teams although we were just a group of young lads who wanted to play as many games at the weekend as possible. When I was growing up I would play at least three games most Saturdays and Sundays and it didn't really bother me that some of the matches were against grown men.

We were only sixteen although I remember my mum drafting in two of my uncles to give us a bit of experience and to make sure we weren't intimidated. The game sticks in my mind because I had a bad back at the time and was really struggling to walk. I was determined not to miss out but after a couple of minutes I took a punch in the ribs and there was just no way I could continue. I was doubled up in agony and had to walk off, much to the disgust of my mum who called me a wimp and a softy. She did say sorry to me after the game!

There must have been about 2000 people crammed into a public park for the game and the crowd were giving me pelters. Most of them had just left the pub and were pissed to start with, but by the time the game went into extra-time they could hardly stand. We eventually scored to go 1-0 ahead and the fans from the pub started yelling and swearing at all the young lads in our team. They were threatening to break our legs if we won and Mum wasn't having any of it. She started giving them a ticking off but that just made them angrier and before too long they were calling her every name under the sun.

Dad was standing beside her with my little sister, Tina, who was still in her pram. Mum then took an umbrella out of the pushchair and whacked this big geezer across the head. That was the cue for all hell to break loose and before I knew it there was a full-scale riot in progress. The police arrived mob-handed and Mum was arrested along with a whole host of undesirables.

It wasn't funny at the time and she was mortified about what happened. Looking back it brings a huge smile to my face every time I think about that incident. The pub team tried to bully a bunch of 16-year-olds and their female manager, but they came off second best – on and off the pitch.

Mum treated all her players like one of her own and they respected her. I think that's why so many of them stayed with our team for years and years. Dad, her trusted number two, was also football daft. He was a Southampton fan who used to go and watch every game that wasn't on a Saturday. That was his busiest day on the market stall and there was no way he could afford to lose any takings.

We never missed any Southampton midweek games and we used to go to the same place every time. Dad would stand right at the corner flag and I would lie on top of a little wall just in front of him. The old Dell was a fantastic ground and I remember watching some great matches when I was a kid. It was the era of Mick Channon, Terry Payne and Bobby Stokes and every night I dreamed of becoming a professional footballer just like them.

As a local lad I had a real soft spot for the Saints although I was actually an Everton supporter. They were my number one team. Colin Harvey was my favourite player when I was a kid but I also thought Joe Royle was different class as well. Liverpool was a long way from Southampton although my dad took me on the train to watch them a couple of times when I was 14 and I really appreciated that.

Both of my parents were always really supportive as I attempted to fulfil a lifelong ambition of playing football for a living. And if it hadn't been for them moving house when I was 11 years old so I could attend a better school then I doubt whether I would have eventually made it.

After I'd left junior school, Alex Perkins, the head teacher at Weston Park Boys' School, approached my mum and asked if she'd consider sending me there. Alex also ran all the youth teams at Southampton and he felt if I attended his school, where there was a real emphasis on sport, rather than the local secondary, I would have a better chance of becoming a footballer. So the whole family moved to Weston just for the sake of me.

You hear all these horror stories about boys-only schools back then, but I loved every minute and was never subjected to any unsavoury rituals. There were a few crackpots in the school though, and I remember a lad called Tony Little dangling one of the teachers out of a second-floor window by her ankles. But, mostly, the discipline was pretty good.

My main memories are of playing sport every day and while I wasn't very academic I did at least gain two GCSEs in English and Maths. I left school at 16 on the Friday afternoon and on the Monday morning I started work as a welder's mate. I hated every minute of it and after four days I quit. I signed on the dole for £12 a week but I was confident I would be offered an apprenticeship at Southampton.

I'd been training with them twice a week for the previous four years after Alex had recommended me and I'd always had plenty of positive feedback from all the different coaches I worked under. During the summer holidays the club always held a series of trial matches to determine which lads would be taken on at the start of the following season. Lawrie McMenemy was the manager at that time and when he came along to the final trial I had an absolute shocker.

For some strange reason they played me on the right wing. I'd never ever played in that position before and, while I was quite quick in those days, I failed to do myself justice. In the space of 90 minutes I felt four years go to waste and I was prepared for the worst when Lawrie took me aside after the match.

'We're not taking you on, son. We don't think you will ever make it as a professional footballer,' he said. Those words crushed me and I felt as if my whole world had collapsed.

Rejection is hard to take at the best of times, but when you are only 16 it's almost impossible to accept. I cried my eyes out for days afterwards until Mum told me to get a grip and stop feeling sorry for myself.

I was signing on every week and playing for her team when I got a call from Stuart Morgan asking if I would like to join Bournemouth. He'd watched me a few times playing in midfield and reckoned I had all the attributes to play as a striker. Stuart was in charge of the youths while Harry Redknapp was the reserve team manager at that time. As my options were pretty limited, I didn't have to think twice about signing.

For the first time in my life I played up front and I scored a stack of goals during the last two thirds of the season. I thoroughly enjoyed training with Stuart, who is one of the best coaches I've ever worked under, and I was delighted to be told I was getting kept on for another year. But then disaster struck at the end of the season when Bournemouth ran into financial trouble and decided to scrap their entire youth set-up. For the second time in the space of twelve months I found myself on the dole with my dreams in tatters.

Mercifully, I didn't have too much time to mope about as within a couple of days Stuart fixed me up with Portsmouth and I continued my apprenticeship at Fratton Park. Ian St John was the manager and Ray Crawford was the youth team boss. Ray was a great guy and I thoroughly enjoyed my time under him. Pompey had a decent reputation for producing good young players back then and I really felt I improved as a player during my time on the south coast. I had to be up at the crack of dawn every morning to get the train down to Portsmouth for training and I had an even earlier start at weekends when we played our games, but I loved it.

On Saturdays I had to help my dad on his stall which meant I had to get up at 3am.

We'd head to the market to buy fresh fruit and veg and after setting up his stall I would catch the 7.30am train to Porstmouth. I didn't think much of it at the time and it certainly didn't affect my football. In my first season with Portsmouth I scored 49 goals and the manager was so impressed he offered me a new contract.

I couldn't believe it when he was sacked during the summer although his successor Jimmy Dickinson assured me I would be part of his plans. Jimmy told me he'd heard great things and, as he wanted to have a look for himself, I was handed my debut in a pre-season friendly at Aldershot.

I was made up at the chance of playing for the first team, but the excitement quickly turned to despair just 45 seconds after coming on as a half-time substitute. I'd just had my first touch and after controlling the ball and turning away from one defender a guy called Joe Jopling – I'll never forget his name – came steaming in late and clattered my left ankle. It was a horrendous challenge and immediately I knew it was broken. I was taken to hospital and put into plaster.

The following day I hobbled into the ground on my crutches as I had a pre-arranged meeting with Jimmy to sign my new deal. However, because the club couldn't be certain I would make a full recovery from my injury the contract offer was withdrawn. Portsmouth said I could continue to use the gym facilities during my rehabilitation although that was scant consolation as I struggled to accept my third knock-back in as many years. I was absolutely gutted and for the first time I started to think that maybe this wasn't meant to be.

I began to consider an alternative career and because money was so tight I got a job as a fitter's mate in a Southampton oil refinery. My job was to climb up the outside of the huge tankers, which were well over 150 feet tall, and replace the old pipes. It used to take the best part of a year to completely refit the tankers as my boss always told me not to rush. He wanted to make sure we all got paid as much overtime as possible so I wasn't complaining. In a good week I could earn as much as £250, which was a good wage at that time, and on top of that I had a small income coming in from football.

After leaving Portsmouth I signed for Dorchester Town, who played in the Southern Premier League, and I continued to make a name for myself as a goalscorer. The standard wasn't great, but for the first time in my life I had a few quid in my pocket and I liked it at Dorchester because they were a good bunch of lads.

Off the pitch things were also going well. At the ripe old age of 19 I got married to my childhood sweetheart, Ann, and we bought our first house together. But she wasn't happy when I told her we couldn't go on honeymoon because I had three games the following week. I think she understood football had to come first as, despite suffering so many set-backs, I still hadn't given up on my dream of becoming a professional.

However, my older brother Stephen didn't quite see things in the same way.

His wedding clashed with an FA Cup qualifying match against Bridport. Victory would earn us a place in the competition proper so it was no contest really, much to the disgust of Stephen. If you want to reach the top in any level of sport then you have to adopt a selfish streak and so many sacrifices have to be made. I was disappointed to miss out on the wedding although if I had to make the same decision again I'd still make the same choice.

Stephen took it badly and unfortunately our relationship was never the same again. Still, Dorchester beat Bridport 4-1 and there were a number of scouts at the match to run the rule over me now that my injury problems were firmly behind me.

One of the interested parties was my old boss Stuart Morgan, now in charge of Weymouth. Weymouth were in the Gola League, which is now the Conference, and I was keen to play at a higher level. I was operating on a non-contract basis at Dorchester which basically meant I got more money and didn't have to pay as much tax. It benefited the club, but the only downside was that they wouldn't get any money if somebody else wanted to sign me.

Weymouth knew this and Stuart was keen to exploit the loophole. I met him and chairman Bill Bowring and I was impressed with everything they had to say. They both had big ambitions for Weymouth and after I agreed terms I was waiting in the boardroom for them to sort out the paperwork when two directors came up to me and said: 'We don't want any of you Dorchester lot down here.' There had always been a rivalry between the two clubs and while I wasn't sure if the two directors were half-joking, I asked Stuart if it was OK to speak with my wife before signing.

After speaking to Ann I decided I couldn't be bothered with the hassle so I told Stuart what had happened and why I'd changed my mind. He said he would get the matter sorted out although by then Dorchester had offered to increase my wages so I opted to remain where I was. Two months later Stuart made another approach and when Weymouth tabled a £6,000 bid, Dorchester, much to my surprise, accepted it. I was on my way.

My debut for Weymouth went pretty well. I scored against Worcester in the FA Cup although I wondered what I'd let myself in for when we played Barrow-in-Furness the following weekend. I had to work at the oil refinery on the Friday morning and after starting at 6am the coach picked me up in Southampton at midday for the marathon trek to Barrow.

We arrived at 10pm that night and after a quick meal headed off to bed. I scored the only goal of the game in a 1-0 win to make the trip worthwhile and then we headed for home immediately afterwards. The journey back took another ten hours and I was in the house only a matter of minutes before I had to rush out the door to begin my Sunday shift at 6am. Combining two jobs was a real struggle and when you consider we trained twice a week in Weymouth, which was also a 90-minute drive from my home, and that we usually played two games, I was constantly shattered. There were some weeks when my wife barely saw me.

As well as moving clubs I also changed jobs, although switching to the docks at Vosper wasn't my smartest decision. The good thing about working at the refinery was that you were outside in the fresh air ninety per cent of the time. But at the shipyards I could go for weeks in the middle of winter without seeing daylight! I'd go to work at 6am when it was pitch black, spend all day refitting the boats and when I reappeared on deck at 4.30pm it was dark again. I'd travel to training and when I woke up the following day the sun was still asleep.

It did get you down and there were plenty of occasions when I considered packing it all in. But, I just kept telling myself that if you want something badly enough then you have to work exceptionally hard to get it. Young footballers today don't know they're born and maybe that's the reason there isn't the same hunger and desire amongst players. Looking back I think my upbringing and the battle I had to endure to fulfil my ambitions contributed a great deal to the success I enjoyed later in my career.

Joining Weymouth was the making of me and so was the decision by Stuart to move me back into midfield. It was Stuart's idea to convert me into a forward although as I developed as a player and became physically more mature he felt I could offer a lot more in the middle of the park. Stuart was right – he usually was – and within a few weeks of joining Weymouth we regularly had a load of scouts from the football league clubs at our matches.

Third Division Oxford were the first to declare their hand, but Weymouth rejected an offer of £20,000, which was a huge amount of money for a non-league outfit. A couple of months later, in March 1980, Stuart called me into his office and said the club had accepted a £30,000 bid from West Bromwich Albion. I knew they had been watching me because I'd spotted their manager, Ron Atkinson, at one of our games against Telford when I went to take a throw-in. I was actually at the Hawthorns for signing talks when Stuart called the Midlands club and asked to speak me.

When I picked up the receiver, I couldn't believe what I was hearing. Stuart informed me that Spurs had matched West Brom's offer. I later found out that White Hart Lane legend Bill Nicholson was the man behind the deal.

Remarkably Bill, who led Spurs to the double in 1961, was en route to Swindon to watch a midfielder when the match was called off. He was standing at the railway station when a guy recognised him and started chatting. As the conversation progressed and Bill explained he was now scouting for Spurs, the bloke suggested he would be better off checking out a youngster at Weymouth. Incredibly, Bill took him at his word and arrived on the south coast to watch our game with Nuneaton. Fortunately I had a blinder and when he went back to White Hart Lane on the Monday he told Keith Burkinshaw I was certainly worth pursuing.

However, by this stage I was all set to commit my future to West Brom. The deal was ninety per cent agreed when I received Stuart's telephone call. My head was spinning and I didn't know what to do for the best. I'd been impressed by the set-up at the Hawthorns and my wife had her heart set on moving to the Midlands. The club had bent over backwards to make her feel at home and they'd also sorted us out with a beautiful house as part of my signing-on package.

Big Ron's sales pitch had pretty much convinced me that joining West Brom would be a smart career choice, yet there was still something nagging away at the back of my mind. Ten per cent of me wasn't convinced and when Spurs made their approach it only added to my indecision. I was actually in Big Ron's office when I took the phone call from Weymouth. When I told him I wanted to give Spurs the courtesy of speaking to them he went ballistic. He told me I was making the biggest mistake of my life and that if I didn't sign the contract immediately then the deal was off the table.

When I stuck to my guns, he locked me in his office and told me I wasn't getting out until I'd put pen to paper. I thought he was joking at first, but I was still in there ninety minutes later. Ron eventually calmed down enough to let me out and I headed straight down to London.

Tottenham put me up in at the Royal Chase Hotel in Enfield and I travelled into the ground on the Friday morning. I met

Keith for the first time and he introduced me to the players. I was completely starstruck as I looked around the dressing room and saw people like Glenn Hoddle, Ricky Villa, Ossie Ardiles and Steve Perryman sitting there. Keith asked me if I wanted to do a light training stint with the lads and I couldn't get changed quick enough. This was the moment I'd been striving for all my life and I was determined to make a decent first impression.

It all started off well enough with a running session around the pitch and I was quite chuffed with myself when I was able to keep up. After half an hour we moved indoors to a massive games hall to play the traditional Friday morning game of seven-a-side. What followed was one of the most embarrassing and humiliating experiences of my career. I ran around like a headless chicken for over an hour and I honestly don't recall touching the ball once. The manager and all the players must have been thinking 'what the fuck have we bought here?' I could hardly put one foot in front of the other when Keith blew the whistle to signal the end of the game.

It must have been close to 100 degrees inside the gym and the sweat was lashing off me. It felt like I'd lost almost a stone in weight just running around chasing shadows. In the dressing room afterwards all the lads were asking me if I was OK, but I didn't have the energy to speak. I just sat there like a little lost boy and when assistant boss Peter Shreeve came in and said the gaffer wanted to see me in his office, I thought he was certain to give me the old 'thanks, but no thanks, son.'

However, much to my relief, he offered me £185 a week to sign plus another £4000 to help with a deposit on a house. It was actually less money than I was earning at Weymouth because I also had a full-time job, but he could have given me £85 a week after the morning I'd just had and I would have accepted.

Just as I was leaving he turned to me and said: 'Sorry, Graham, but can you tell me what position you play? I've never seen you play, but Bill Nicholson told me you would make it and if that's Bill's opinion then it's good enough for me and good enough for this football club.'

I was totally flabbergasted, but that's how I signed for Spurs.

On the way back to Southampton on the train from Waterloo I argued with Ann for the whole journey. She still wanted me to join West Brom, but after two hours of bickering I finally managed to persuade her that we could make a go of it in London.

The worst part was having to ring up Ron Atkinson and tell him that I had signed for Spurs. He wasn't in the mood for chit-chat and promptly slammed the phone down as soon as the words were out of my mouth. I took his reaction as a compliment because he obviously wanted me that much and that filled me with plenty of hope and optimism for the challenge at White Hart Lane. And after my inauspicious first training session, I needed every ounce of self-belief in my body.

It was a massive step up coming from the Gola League where I was up against part-time outfits every week, but I'd always thought I was a decent footballer. I just needed to improve my touch because that's what separates good players from great players.

A couple of weeks after signing, Keith took me on the end of season tour to Austria and I played in a couple of friendly matches. The emphasis was more on drinking than football, however the trip was the perfect ice-breaker for me and it helped me get to know my team-mates for the following pre-season.

There was a big fuss when I signed because at £30,000 I was the most expensive recruit ever to come from non-league football. But, that fee really paled into insignificance alongside Spurs' two main summer signings – Steve Archibald, who cost £800,000 from Aberdeen and Garth Crooks, who arrived from Stoke in a £600,000 move.

Understandably, all the media attention was on them and that suited me just fine. It allowed me to go about my business quietly and with the minimum of fuss. Just the way I liked it.

Given the abundance of talent at the manager's disposal I knew it would be a while before I got a crack at the first team, but I wanted to make sure I made the right impression when we reported back after the summer break.

Ironically, we went to Scotland on a pre-season tour where I saw Ibrox for the first time. Spurs played Rangers in a friendly to commemorate the opening of a new stand. We had a couple of games but I wasn't involved in any of them. The trip north gave me a taste of what it was like to be part of the top team set-up and I knew this was the life I wanted.

Sometimes I felt as if I had to pinch myself because I was sharing a dressing with guys like Hoddle, Villa and Ardiles. Back then they were the equivalent of what Frank Lampard, Cristiano Ronaldo and Fernando Torres are today, yet I never felt intimidated when I was amongst them. Everybody at the club made me feel welcome and the encouragement I received from the first moment I walked into White Hart Lane was magnificent.

As I'd taken a pay cut to join Spurs I couldn't afford to furnish my new house in Nazeing. It cost £27,500 and I was skint after taking out a big mortgage. Thankfully, Gerry Armstrong came to the rescue and bailed me out with a huge favour. His mate had a furniture and fittings shop and he arranged to carpet my whole house for nothing. I squared up with him later when I finally came into a bit of cash. Gerry was a great lad although a bit eccentric. I remember he used to cycle ten miles in to training in the morning, do his session, and then cycle back home again.

The majority of the players at Spurs when I signed were world-class performers, top internationals from around the globe. I was a country bumpkin who'd just arrived from Weymouth. Yet I was overwhelmed by the faith shown in me by the manager and my team-mates and I was determined to repay them. Steve Perryman was different class and he would often stay behind after training to do some extra work with me.

It didn't seem like much at the time as I always did a couple of extra hours training on my own every day. But, when I got older I realised those two or three hours Steve devoted to me every week were an invaluable part of my development. And I will be eternally grateful for that as he played a major part in helping me achieve so much in football.

The first few months flew past in a blur and while I felt I was making huge progress any chance of making my big breakthrough appeared a long way off. That season Spurs were heavily touted as genuine title contenders and given the amount of money Keith had spent bringing in two strikers, there was a real buzz around North London.

The supporters believed we were capable of breaking Liverpool's dominance and after a bright start the optimism levels on the terraces soared even further. However, consistency has never been Spurs' strong suit and the inevitable run of poor results duly followed. Bad news for the fans, but great news for myself as I was handed my debut months sooner than expected.

It came against Stoke City when I came on with a couple of minutes to go. After all the rejections and the long struggle to make it to the top it was a terrific moment, not just for me, but also for my family. Suddenly, I felt all the years of hard graft and toil were worth it. Those couple of minutes also proved I was right to pursue my childhood dream of becoming a professional footballer.

But there was no time to rest on my laurels and a couple of weeks later I sampled my first North London derby. I quickly realised that beating Arsenal means more to Spurs fans than anything else in the world and my opportunity to put one over on our biggest rivals came in a League Cup clash at Highbury. I replaced Ricky Villa for the last half an hour of a 1-0 victory and, to this day, I couldn't tell you anything about the match. There was a capacity crowd at White Hart Lane and the atmosphere was incredible. That's all I remember. The game just completely passed me by. It was like my first training session in the gym all over again and while I'm sure I did touch the ball this time, I've no recollection. I must have done something right because the gaffer came up to me after the game, gave me a big pat on the back and told me I'd played well. I had to take his word for it. Even though I couldn't quantify my contribution, I still felt twenty feet tall after being part of the team who beat Arsenal.

Another spell in the reserves brought me back down to earth before the moment I'd been desperately waiting for arrived on December 6, 1980 following another spell of poor results. The opposition was Liverpool, the First Division champions and league leaders, and the venue was Anfield, where Spurs hadn't won since 1912. No pressure then.

I was only called into the squad after training on Friday morning because Terry Yorath was an injury doubt. I actually felt quite guilty as I was the one responsible for crocking Terry. We were both going for a ball during a game of seven-a-sides when I accidently pushed him into the gym wall. He put his hands out to stop himself and crushed three of his fingers in the process. At the time Terry didn't make much of it and while it was obvious he'd hurt himself, he was confident that a bucket of ice and a couple of painkillers would see him alright. The club doctor gave him a painkilling injection and we set off on the coach journey to Merseyside on Friday afternoon.

By sheer coincidence, Terry was my room-mate at the time and in the middle of the night he was in so much pain he had to call out the doctor to give him another injection. His condition deteriorated even further and on the Saturday morning he was rushed to hospital for an emergency operation on his hand.

After breakfast I was summoned to the manager's room. I was bracing myself for a bollocking for putting Terry in hospital. Instead the gaffer told me I was starting against

19

Liverpool – at right back. I'd never played there before in my life and secretly I still fancied myself as a striker even though Spurs bought me to play in the middle of the park. The reason Keith deployed me at the back was because he thought the pace of the game in midfield might catch me out given my lack of experience. Back then it didn't get much harder than a trip to Merseyside and it was the equivalent of going to either Old Trafford or Stamford Bridge today. So Steve Perryman was moved into the middle of the park to accommodate me at full back.

I was shaking like a leaf when I was in the tunnel but as soon as the game got underway the nerves disappeared and I thoroughly enjoyed the experience. The Liverpool team was frightening and packed full of top-class talent. I was up against people like Ray Kennedy, Terry McDermott, Kenny Dalglish, Alan Hansen, Sammy Lee and Ronnie Whelan but, strangely, I never felt intimidated. We lost 2-1 but we gave a good account of ourselves and the manager told me he was delighted with my performance afterwards.

I'd never ever doubted my ability during the long struggle to reach the top although it was those ninety minutes at Anfield that filled me with the self-belief which carried me throughout my career. On my full debut I'd played out of position, away from home, against the best team in the country and I didn't look out of place.

I kept my place in the team for the next few games and due to an injury crisis Keith asked me if I could play in central defence against Aston Villa a couple of weeks later. I think it was actually Peter Shreeve's idea because he reckoned I had all the attributes to develop into a decent centre half. I was strong in the air, I could tackle and my distribution was excellent. So I partnered Paul Miller against Villa and we retained our places until the end of the season. We struck up an instant rapport and we just flourished together.

My first brush with controversy as a player came in a match against Bobby Robson's Ipswich just before Christmas. They were flying high at the top of the table alongside Liverpool and their front three of Alan Brazil, Eric Gates and Paul Mariner was regarded as the best strike force in England. The match was played in some of the worst conditions I ever experienced with sleet and gale force winds making it almost impossible to play decent football.

It was a real war of attrition, a survival of the fittest and we wanted to show Ipswich we could hold our own against anybody at The Lane. The tackles were flying in everywhere and while we eventually triumphed 5-3 in a bad-tempered affair, the win was overshadowed by an incident involving me and Eric Gates. The Ipswich striker wasn't impressed when I constantly invaded his space and never allowed him a second's respite, and after a few squabbles he was eventually red-carded after taking a swipe at me.

I remember landing on top of him as we jumped for a high ball, but it was simply my momentum that had carried me forward. Gates was having none of it and accused me of trampling on him. As I protested my innocence he threw a haymaker which, thankfully, I managed to avoid. But the referee spotted it and sent him for an early bath. The Ipswich players were seething and a furious Bobby Robson blamed me in the media afterwards for getting Gates sent off.

It was the first of many scrapes I'd get myself involved in although I still maintain I was the innocent party. One thing was for certain. I was now in the big time and loving every single minute of it.

2

OSSIE'S DREAM

Inconsistency quickly put paid to our hopes of mounting a serious championship challenge in season 1980–81, but Spurs have always been a club synonymous with the FA Cup and we were still optimistic about our chances of putting together a decent run in the competition. On paper we had a team capable of matching anyone on our day and we knew that if the draw was kind to us then we had a genuine shot of reaching Wembley.

I'd only ever played in the qualifying stages of the FA Cup before so to go straight into the hat for the third round was the furthest I'd ever been without kicking a ball. First up for us was a tricky trip to Loftus Road and while we rode our luck in a scoreless draw we had little trouble despatching QPR 3-1 in the replay. Tony Galvin was outstanding that night and I remember him winning the game for us almost single-handedly.

Tony joined the club at the same time as me and, coincidentally, he also came from non-league football. He arrived from Goole Town after finishing his university course where he studied Russian. I roomed with him then and I remember him practising it all the time. The other players used to say his

Russian was easier to understand than his Goole accent. But, while he was also the cleverest player I've ever come across, he was also one of the most under-rated. On his day, Tony was virtually unplayable and within the space of six months both Tony and myself had gone from being part-timers to first team regulars with one of the biggest clubs in the country.

Looking back, it was an incredible fairytale and you just couldn't see that happening in the Premiership now. Can you imagine Juande Ramos or Luiz Felipe Scolari scouring the lower leagues in England for new players? It wouldn't happen in a million years which makes our achievements back then all the more remarkable. Around the same time people like Stuart Pearce, Andy Townsend and Cyril Regis followed the same path from non-league and managed to carve out decent careers for themselves in the professional game. I'm sure there are players who are capable of making the step up now although they will never get the same opportunity that was afforded me and Tony. Sadly, those days seem to be long gone.

Despite not having the same pedigree as most of my new team-mates, they couldn't have made me feel more welcome in those early days at Spurs. The dressing room might have been a who's who of international superstars, yet almost every one of them went out of their way to make me feel an integral part of the club. They were a great bunch and one of the friendliest was Steve Archibald. A lot of people might find that hard to believe as Steve had, and still has, a reputation for being a surly character, an arrogant loner who could start an argument in an empty house. It's a tag which has stuck with him since his playing days but he really looked after me in the early days when I joined Spurs.

There was a real sense of togetherness within the squad at that time, with everyone pulling in the same direction, and it was that unity which helped us bring the club their first trophy in twenty years. In the fourth round of the cup the draw was again kind to us with Third Division Hull City providing the opposition at White Hart Lane. The game should have been a formality although, to their credit, they made us struggle until Garry Brooke grabbed the opening goal five minutes from time. Archibald secured the victory when he doubled our advantage at the death.

Another home draw in the fifth round saw a Coventry team, who had a teenage Mark Hateley in their ranks, arrive in London. But, to be perfectly honest, they were a beaten side before they even stepped foot on the pitch. Four days earlier, Coventry's young team suffered a crushing blow when they surrendered a one-goal lead in the second leg of the League Cup semi-final against West Ham to narrowly miss out on a trip to Wembley. They looked a bedraggled bunch when they rolled up at White Hart Lane and we comfortably saw them off 3-1 to book our place in the quarter final.

This was the third time in as many years we had been to this stage of the tournament although the previous two attempts to go further had both ended in failure. However, when we were paired with Exeter City, every one of us knew we would never get a better opportunity to end our quarter final hoodoo.

The Third Division minnows had already claimed the scalps of Newcastle and Leicester although we didn't think for one moment they would pose us any problems. Of course, publicly you have to say the right things and pay them plenty of respect, but privately the lads were jumping for joy and expecting to hammer five or six past Exeter. It didn't quite turn out like that and when the score was still 0-0 at the interval, the natives were beginning to get restless. Eventually we managed to ease the crowd's nerves when we broke the deadlock midway through the second half courtesy of a goal from yours truly. I nodded home a Glenn Hoddle free-kick before my central defensive partner Paul Miller sealed a hard-fought 2-0 victory and took us to within 90 minutes of a place in the FA Cup Final.

Wolves, Manchester City and Ipswich joined us in the hat and we were all desperate to land the team from the Midlands. Lady Luck was again smiling on us when we got the draw we were hoping for.

The game was played at Hillsborough and we travelled north on the Friday night. When we arrived at our hotel in the city centre there must have been about 2000 supporters outside signing songs and waving banners. They provided us with a terrific reception and one we really appreciated, but they were still making so much noise long after midnight that Keith had to get out of his bed and ask them to be quiet so the players could all get some sleep. But, despite the fans upholding their part of the bargain to help us get some much needed shut-eye it didn't make any difference to me. There were so many thoughts flashing through my mind that I found it impossible to doze off. A few months ago I was an everyday Joe who played part-time football with Weymouth and here I was just 90 minutes away from fulfilling a boyhood dream of playing in an FA Cup Final. It was real Roy of the Rovers stuff as far as I was concerned and no matter how hard I tried I just couldn't get the occasion out of my mind.

Eventually I got up just after 6am and by 7am I was walking aimlessly around the streets of Sheffield. But I wasn't alone. I had Glenn Hoddle, John Lacy and my room-mate Milija Alexsic for company. Through a mixture of nerves, adrenalin, excitement and pressure none of us could sleep. My stomach was churning and I didn't each much for breakfast or lunch and it was a relief when we finally began the coach journey to the stadium. When we arrived at Hillsborough there were 35,000 Spurs fans there and it felt just like White Hart Lane. The reception we got helped take away the jitters and when referee Clive Thomas blew his whistle to get the game underway, all the tension disappeared.

We were strong favourites to win although I knew it wouldn't be easy as I was up against Andy Gray, who was one of the toughest centre forward's around. Strong and physical, Andy was no shrinking violet on a football pitch and it was my job to keep him quiet. Thankfully we managed to get off to a great start with Steve Archibald giving us the lead after just four minutes. Kenny Hibbitt equalised for Wolves then Glenn put us back in front just before the break with a stunning trademark free-kick which he curled into the top corner. In the second half Wolves never had a shot on goal and I just couldn't see them scoring in a million years. But with seconds remaining, they were awarded a dubious penalty. Hibbitt was fouled outside the area by, of all people, Glenn, but he kept running and eventually went down inside the box.

Unfortunately for us the referee was the only person in the

entire stadium who reckoned it was a penalty. Clive relished being in the limelight and he just loved giving controversial decisions and while we protested vehemently it was to no avail. Willie Carr slotted it away and the match went into extra-time.

Mentally we were shot to pieces and as I looked around, all the players were slumped in the centre circle with their heads in their hands. From being virtually in the final we were there for the taking and if it hadn't been for Paul Miller then Wolves would have beaten us that afternoon. Maxi was the only player who kept his concentration and the only member of the team who didn't look physically and mentally drained. He somehow managed to carry ten of us for another 30 minutes, yet, to this day, I still don't know how Wolves failed to score. They'd missed a glorious opportunity and when the replay came around I knew we would be heading to Wembley.

The game was at Highbury which was almost like a home match for us and the final nail in Wolves' coffin was the loss of Andy Gray through injury. That news provided us with another boost and when Garth Crooks scored early doors I knew we would win comfortably. Garth scored again, but it was Ricky Villa who really stole the show that night. He was at his mesmerising best and his second-half wonder goal was the cue for some unforgettable celebrations at the home of our biggest rivals.

At the final whistle, we couldn't get off the pitch because the fans invaded it. They were not going to let a special moment like this pass without making the most of it. They didn't go quite as far as digging up the turf like the Tartan Army did after Scotland beat England at Wembley in 1977, but they did wreck the goalposts. I also knew a few people who nicked the corner flags for souvenirs. I had my shorts and shirt ripped off me but was on such a high at reaching my first major final that I was almost oblivious to what was going on.

Things were not much clearer the following morning when I woke up with the mother of all hangovers. The lads celebrated until 4am and I don't think beer has ever tasted as sweet as it did that night. When I eventually sobered up the realisation that I was going to be playing against Manchester City in an FA Cup Final at Wembley suddenly dawned on me. I was living the dream.

The build-up to the big day was terrific and the senior players like Steve Perryman and Glenn Hoddle kept telling me to make sure I took it all in as this might be the one and only time you get an opportunity like this in your career. The pre-match hype all started when Chas and Dave, who were massive Spurs fans, approached the club about making a Cup Final record. Keith put the suggestion to all the lads and while none of us could really sing we were all up for it, big style.

I remember going along to a recording studio in Portland Street where we all got tanked up and thrashed out the song in a couple of hours. It was a great laugh making the video with Chas and Dave, who didn't take themselves too seriously, and within 48 hours 'Ossie's Dream' was in the shops. To this day I can still remember all the words and every time I hear the song it brings a huge smile to my face. It's one of those catchy tunes that just stays with you forever.

Incredibly, it flew off the shelves in Cup Final week and reached number four in the charts. There must have been thousands of football pop songs over the years with 99 per cent of them instantly forgettable. But, alongside New Order's 'World in Motion', England's World Cup song at Italia 90, 'Ossie's Dream' is arguably the one that most football fans remember best. And while it was never going to win us any Brit Awards we did make appearances on *Top of the Pops* and *Blue Peter*.

It was good fun and the publicising of the song was a welcome diversion as it helped take the pressure off the squad before we faced Man City. The song was, in part, a tribute to Ossie Ardiles and most of the focus was centred around the little Argentine World Cup winner and fellow countryman, Ricky Villa.

To be honest, the rest of the lads didn't mind that at all because, again, it allowed us to go about our business quietly and prepare for the biggest game of our lives without too many distractions. On the Tuesday before the final we had an Open Day where the supporters were invited to watch us train and on the Wednesday there was a press day when the media from around the world descended on White Hart Lane. The following day we travelled to the Ponsbourne Hotel, which would be our base for the next 48 hours. On Friday the entire squad gathered in the hotel lounge and the BBC did a live link-up to Argentina allowing Ossie and Ricky to speak with their parents.

That night I was tucked up in bed by 10pm, but, yet again, I couldn't sleep. I must have been up at least five times during the night and by 6am I was strolling around the gardens of the hotel. It was a beautiful morning and I wandered about for an hour before heading back up to my room for a shower. I spent the next couple of hours reading the papers and then went for breakfast with the rest of the boys at 8.30am. Keith had already named the starting line-up on the Thursday and given everybody their instructions so the team meeting was quite brief as everything had already been said. After a light lunch we got on the bus and made the 45-minute journey to the national stadium.

The route was lined with blue and white and everywhere you looked there were Spurs supporters. It seemed like we passed hundreds of thousands of them on the way to the ground and that coach trip filled me with an enormous sense of pride prior to kick-off.

I was nervous. I was only 21 at the time and, in reality, I was bricking it. But, at the same time, I was chomping at the bit to get on the pitch. This was what I'd dreamed about for the past 15 years and I was determined not to let the occasion pass by without making a contribution.

The first half was certainly memorable, but for all the wrong reasons. The dream threatened quickly to turn into a nightmare for both Spurs and Graham Roberts. We were so sluggish at the beginning of the game and it didn't come as any great surprise when City took the lead through a Tommy Hutchison header. That was a sore one to take, but not half as painful as what was just about to follow.

First I almost knocked myself unconscious when I accidentally butted the back of Kevin Reeves and split my head wide open. I was seeing stars and had blood streaming down my face, yet you didn't have to go off the pitch in those days so I just soldiered on hoping I'd quickly feel better. Within a couple of minutes I felt tip-top again although there was more misery in store for me just before the interval.

I can remember stooping to head away a long ball only to catch the flying boot of team-mate Chris Hughton flush in the gob. He knocked me out cold and there was claret everywhere. The game was held up for about five minutes until I regained consciousness and received treatment from the doctors. When I eventually came round I felt this weird sensation in my mouth. The pain was excruciating and I'd never experienced anything like it in my life.

It turned out I'd lost two of my front teeth and another one had been cracked in half. The nerves were all exposed and this was the worst ever toothache multiplied by one hundred. I was in agony, but somehow, after being cleaned up a little bit, I managed to stagger through the last few minutes until half-time. During the interval Keith consulted the doc, who told him there was no way I could possibly continue so Gary Brooke was instructed to get stripped and start warming-up. At that moment I sneaked off to the toilet, popped a couple of paracetamols and went back out on the pitch. The gaffer was looking for me everywhere and when he came back out for the start of the second half I refused to go off. In the end he had no option but to let me stay on. I might have been suffering the worst pain imaginable but there was just no way I was giving up after 45 minutes. In the dressing room I'd felt really faint and I was worried I might pass out again, but once I got some fresh air in my lungs I felt much better.

Somehow I managed to see out the rest of the 90 minutes and extra-time. Hutchison might have been the City hero in the first half, but after the break he wrote his name into the history books by becoming the first player to score for both teams in an FA Cup Final. He deflected a Glenn Hoddle free-kick into his own net to hand us a precious lifeline and give us another crack at lifting the Cup in the replay five days later.

To be honest we barely deserved it as they stifled us in the middle of the park and didn't allow Glenn, Ossie or Ricky to get on the ball and dictate play. Ricky had a shocker and when he was substituted he stormed off up the tunnel in tears. He looked a broken man when we came into the dressing room after the match.

There was no in-between with Ricky. He was either brilliant or anonymous and he was so upset because he thought he'd let everybody down. The game was also being screened live in Argentina and I think he was so eager to impress that the whole occasion just got to him. In contrast, his replacement, Gary Brooke, had a blinder when he came on and the whole squad just presumed he would start in the replay. But Keith proved just what a great manager he was in the aftermath of that first game with City. When he came into the dressing room the first thing he did was go up to Ricky and put his arm around him. In his thick Yorkshire brogue he said: 'Don't worry, Ricky. You will be the first name on my teamsheet because I know you will win us the game on Thursday.'

It was a fantastic piece of management because you could see Ricky get an instant lift from it. We also had a massive party planned for the Saturday night at the Royal Lancaster Hotel in London and the players automatically thought it would be cancelled. After all we had nothing to celebrate or commiserate and we needed to prepare for a second game in five days. But Keith was having none of it. The soiree went ahead as planned and everybody got royally pissed. It was another master stroke from the manager.

For me, the drink helped to take away the pain although at the end of the night I felt and looked like Shane McGowan from the Pogues. On the Monday I visited a specialist in Epping and they agreed to operate on the Friday morning. Normally the replay would have been on the Wednesday, but England were playing Brazil at Wembley that evening so our game was scheduled for 24 hours later. The first match was a pretty dull affair, but the second remains one of the most memorable FA Cup Finals ever. It was an all-time classic, a game which leaves you breathless just talking about it.

This time we couldn't have got off to a better start with Ricky instantly repaying the faith shown in him by the manager and giving us an early advantage. Our lead didn't last long though as Steve McKenzie scored a wonder goal. It was a stunning 20-yard volley into the top corner and even to this day, I don't think I've ever seen a shot struck as sweetly as that.

Amazingly, it wasn't even the best goal on the night.

The score remained 1-1 until half-time although ten minutes after the restart City went ahead as Chris Hughton and Paul Miller combined to bring down Dave Bennett. Kevin Reeves slotted home from the spot although despite trailing I was always confident we would get back in the contest.

It was a real end-to-end match and when Garth Crooks drew us level with 20 minutes remaining I started to think our name was on the trophy. Of course I couldn't envisage what was to follow as Ricky made amends for his poor showing in the first game with arguably the most famous goal in the history of the competition. Nobody ever remembers this but I actually began the move, making a block tackle on the edge

34

of my own box before playing a 40-yard pass to Tony Galvin on the left wing. Tony cut back onto his right foot and played a square pass in to Ricky. There were a clutch of City players surrounding him although you could see them all backing off. I don't know if they were scared to make a tackle in such a dangerous area so late in the game, but Ricky sensed their panic and just kept going, and going. He danced this way and that way and after gliding effortlessly past four defenders he coolly slotted the ball under Joe Corrigan.

I never tire of watching that goal because it was sheer poetry in motion. Ricky ran to the dug-out to celebrate and although we ran after him we couldn't catch him. We held out for the remaining ten minutes and when the final whistle sounded I just fell to my knees. I was overwhelmed by emotion and I was struggling to comprehend just what I'd achieved. Twelve months earlier I was combining playing part-time football with Weymouth and working as a fitter in a Southampton dockyard. Now I was walking up the steps at Wembley to receive a winner's medal from Princess Michael of Kent. From being a nobody, suddenly I felt like royalty.

It's incredible to think that match was almost thirty years ago because I can still remember it as if it were yesterday. Looking back, I still feel an enormous sense of pride to have been involved in one of the greatest ever FA Cup Finals. Memories like that can't be taken away although I don't recall too much of the following day!

On the Friday morning I was booked in to have my teeth fixed at a private hospital in Epping. My appointment was at 8.30am, although the post-match celebrations hadn't even finished by then. After the game we went back to the

Chanticleer Club at the stadium where we had the mother of all parties. The champagne flowed, and flowed, and flowed and when I finally jumped in a taxi with my wife Ann it was daylight. I'd completely forgotten about my operation, until the hospital called at 11.30am to remind me. As speech was beyond me at this point, Ann explained I was a bit the worse for wear although the doctors told her just to bring me in as soon as possible. Unsurprisingly they dispensed with the general anaesthetic and opted for a local one instead. And while I'm sure they wouldn't have carried out the operation today for fear of being sued, the surgeon didn't seem too concerned that I'd drunk enough alcohol to fill a small swimming pool only a few hours earlier.

He told Ann I should come round within the hour although eight hours later I was still out for the count due to the after effects of the booze. Still wearing the same gear as the night before, I finally surfaced at 8pm on the Friday night. My winner's medal was still in my pocket so the nurses asked me if I would do a tour of the wards. Looking like a cross between Mr Ed and a tramp who'd just been dragged through a bush backwards, I spent the next few hours regaling the patients with stories of the night before and getting my picture taken. It was midnight when I eventually arrived home and even though I'd spent most of the day sleeping I was absolutely shattered and went straight back to bed.

I was still on cloud nine when I woke up the following morning to even more good news. Keith called me into his office to offer me a new contract and hand me a £6,000 bonus payment for winning the FA Cup. As Spurs had doubled my wages to £18,000 a year, I didn't have to think twice about signing it. Money has never been my biggest motivation, but after struggling for so many years I felt like a lottery winner that day as I sat in the manager's office.

I didn't think life could get much better but this was only the beginning.

3

SO NEAR YET SO FAR

Just because it was Spurs' Centenary season, I didn't realise we would play almost 100 games. That's what it felt like when we reached the end of the most exhausting and ultimately disappointing campaign of my entire career. At one stage it looked like we could make history by becoming the first British team to win four major trophies in one season. For so long we were on course for the unprecedented quadruple of First Division Championship, FA Cup, League Cup and European Cup Winner's Cup. Sadly it all ended in heartache and we were fortunate to beat Second Division Queen's Park Rangers in the FA Cup Final after a replay to avoid ending up empty-handed.

There were so many parallels between Spurs' quest for four trophies and Rangers' attempt at winning the Grand Slam last season. I knew exactly how Walter Smith's players felt to be running on empty and still chasing glory on several fronts. Like Rangers, we played more than 70 energy-sapping matches only to lose out on three of our four targets right at the death. At the end we were running on nothing more than adrenalin and we only just managed to stagger over the finishing line in the FA Cup Final at Wembley.

Three decades later I had high hopes Rangers would triumph where Spurs failed, although deep down I feared history would repeat itself. And sure enough, just like we did in the early eighties, my former club hit the wall when the burden of trying to fly the flag both domestically and in Europe proved too much for them. The similarities were uncanny between our two shots at glory and when you are in that situation the mental and physical strain is extremely hard to handle. The football authorities didn't provide Rangers with any help, forcing them to play a ridiculous number of fixtures in a short space of time and at Spurs it was our schedule that also proved our undoing.

We were going for the League along with Everton and Liverpool and I'm convinced we would have won it if we didn't have such a backlog of fixtures. Around the turn of the year we went three weeks without a league fixture because of the weather. That cost us. Then in the space of two months we played 22 games in all competitions. They were all important matches and we simply didn't have the capacity to cope.

A 3-2 victory at the Dell when I scored all three goals, the only senior hat-trick of my career, was one of the few highlights as our league challenge petered out. I don't think any team in world football could cope with a schedule like that regardless of how fit or mentally prepared they are. Losing to Barcelona in the semi-final of the Cup Winner's Cup really knocked the stuffing out of us and when we returned to domestic duties we fell apart. The writing was on the wall when we tossed away a 2-0 lead at home to Sunderland and then failed to win any of our last four games against Man Utd, Liverpool, Notts Forest and Ipswich to only finish third.

That was the closest I ever came to winning a championship in England and the players were devastated.

In April and May we had to play 11 games in 23 days and that was beyond our capabilities. We played more than 70 games that season – 42 in the league alone. It got to a stage where we didn't train for months. We just did a light jog in the morning and then messed about with a game of five-a-side.

We didn't have masseurs, dieticians or a team of medical experts looking after us back then. In fact, after the games we would all get a few pints of lager down us in the players' lounge. That was normal and encouraged by the manager. Somehow I don't think the Rangers players downed pints as part of their preparations for the UEFA Cup Final last season although with Ally McCoist on the coaching staff you never know!

I found it was the closing stages of matches when fatigue unexpectedly crept up on you and sapped all the strength from your legs. Tiredness does not become so much of a factor when you are winning every week although it's an issue when the victories dry up. Our legs just gave in when we drew with Sunderland and I remember leading 2-0 against Liverpool in a vital league match that season. We were knackered in the second half and we were lucky to draw 2-2.

It's in the last 20 minutes of matches where you come unstuck because you put so much effort into the early part of the game and then you tire without warning. We were toiling for the last month of the season but the chance to win a quadruple kept us going. However, when the momentum started to wane I knew we were in trouble. And suddenly from being in the driving seat to win four trophies we almost didn't win any.

The same happened to Rangers, who were fortunate to beat Dundee United in the CIS Cup and then only staggered past Queen of the South in the Scottish Cup Final. If they had been up against any top-flight team at Hampden that day there's no way they would have won.

It was a similar story when we played QPR. By the time we got to Wembley the wins had dried up and we barely had enough ammunition to beat an average Second Division outfit. Like Rangers, we also made it to the League Cup Final in season 1981/82 and the day before we faced Liverpool I had my one and only fall out with Keith Burkinshaw.

I'd played in every game en route to Wembley and had been an ever-present in the team since the previous season. However, completely out of the blue, Keith dropped me for Ricky Villa, who had been out injured for a while. He tried to appease me by telling me that I would play in plenty more cup finals but I wasn't having any of it. It was a big call from Keith as I had been playing well in midfield at the time and there were loads of question marks surrounding Ricky's fitness. Fair play to him for having the balls to make that kind of decision, although I was totally devastated to miss out. You don't realise it at the time because you are so wrapped up in yourself but events like that do make you mentally tougher for the future.

There was only one substitute permitted at that time so I didn't even have the consolation of making the bench. I still sat there with the other members of the squad during the game and I did get a medal, but I didn't feel part of the day in any way whatsoever. We should have won that day and while we actually led up until the final moments of the game, the turning point came after just 15 minutes of the match.

Tony Galvin was having a blinder on the left flank and he was taking the piss out of Liverpool skipper Phil Neal, who was playing at right back. Graeme Souness realised this and the next time Tony went for the ball he hit him like a ton of bricks. For good measure he told Tony he could expect the same every time he touched the ball. I think Tony shat himself and he was about as much use as a chocolate fireguard after that. Souness was a ruthless bastard but he was also clever with it and I believe that tackle, which had Tony limping for the rest of the game, turned the course of the Cup Final.

Stevie Archibald put us 1-0 up but with three minutes remaining he missed an absolute sitter to put the game out of sight and maintain Spurs' record of never having lost a domestic cup final. You'd have put your mortgage on Archie slotting it away, but unfortunately he didn't and that miss would come back to haunt us big style. It was our own fault really as we had been in control although with Tony struggling we just lacked that killer instinct in the final third.

Seconds after Archie's miss, Liverpool went up the park and Ronnie Whelan turned home a David Johnson cross to force the contest into extra-time. The following 30 minutes were a formality for Liverpool as we were mentally gone. Keith was trying his best to gee up the lads although I could see by the look in their eyes he was fighting a losing battle. I felt totally helpless sitting on the sidelines as our dream of winning a Grand Slam evaporated in front of a 100,000-strong Wembley crowd. Whelan's late strike had given them a massive psychological lift and it was no surprise to see him score again in extra-time. Ian Rush netted a third and the trophy was on its way back to Merseyside.

As the season drew towards its conclusion the league title remained our main aim although, being realistic, the FA Cup represented our best chance of securing some silverware. We were preparing for our semi-final clash with Leicester when our plans were plunged into chaos in the most extraordinary of circumstances.

The Falkands crisis had come to the forefront of public consciousness at that time and the day before our game with Leicester, Argentina invaded the British colony. It was a tough and sensitive time for our Argentine players, Ossie Ardiles and Ricky Villa, and also for the manager. Ironically, the semi-final was due to be Ossie's last game for Spurs before heading back to South America to begin Argentina's preparations for the defence of their World Cup crown in Spain that summer.

Keith had a gentleman's agreement with their coach, Cesar Menotti, that Ossie would be released if Spurs reached the FA Cup Final. But given that Britain was now at war with Argentina, I think we all realised that was never going to happen. I felt sorry for Ossie because he was plunged into a diplomatic situation that was beyond his control although he deserves enormous credit for the way he handled it.

Before we played Leicester he was being plagued by phone calls from his homeland pleading him not to play. He was being placed under a lot of pressure from politicians, military men and the Argentinian public, who all wanted him and Ricky to return at the earliest opportunity. However, Ossie ignored them all and played his final game for Spurs that season in the semi-final before flying home.

It was an uncomfortable day for everybody as he was booed and taunted by the Leicester fans every time he touched the ball. Incredibly he didn't let it affect him and he actually set up the opening goal for Garth Crooks. An Ian Wilson own goal doubled our lead and guaranteed we would be appearing in our second successive FA Cup Final.

Ossie wasn't allowed to return for the final although Ricky remained in England. Keith and all the players were 100 per cent behind him and we all wanted him to play against QPR. The whole country had taken Ricky to their hearts following his heroics in the final 12 months before, but I knew he was struggling with his conscience this time round. It was a heart-breaking situation and the fact his homeland had invaded the Falklands was something completely outwith his control.

In my opinion, sport should have nothing to do with politics, although with stories of British servicemen losing their lives dominating the news headlines every night it was impossible to ignore the fact we were in the middle of a war with Argentina. Keith had witnessed Ossie being jeered every time he touched the ball in the semi and he feared Ricky would get the same treatment at Wembley. Ossie was a much stronger character and better equipped to handle it, while Ricky was a sensitive soul and I think he would have crumbled. In the end, after days of deliberating, Keith took the horrible decision to drop Ricky from the team.

Ricky felt even his presence at Wembley would only increase the tension and attract more headlines for the wrong reasons so he stayed at home and watched the match on television.

The first game didn't make for comfortable viewing. It was a shocker, devoid of entertainment and we really struggled to break them down. Terry Venables was in charge of QPR at the time and his teams were always well organised and well drilled.

Still, we were convinced we had done enough when I played in Glenn with ten minutes remaining. His shot took a wicked deflection to completely deceive their keeper, Peter Hucker. However, with time running out, Bob Hazell flicked on a long Simon Stainrod throw-in and Terry Fenwick popped up at the back post to head home the equaliser and force a replay.

Once again the second game was played on a Thursday and while it was better than the first it didn't come close to matching the drama and excitement 12 months previously against Man City. This time Ricky turned up and it was heart-warming to hear the Spurs supporters singing his name. There was so much animosity around at that time, which was perfectly understandable as soldiers and seamen were putting their lives on the line. But the Spurs fans displayed a real human side that night and I know how much their support meant to Ricky at such a difficult time.

The players on the pitch appeared to feed off the feel-good vibe and within six minutes we were ahead. I remember making a deep run from midfield into the penalty box and, out of the corner of my eye, I could see Bob Hazell come charging in like a raging bull. I flicked the ball inside him and, just as I was preparing to shoot, Tony Currie swiped my legs away and the referee pointed to the spot. Glenn tucked the penalty away to provide us with a cushion, which was just as well because QPR murdered us for the next 84 minutes.

The efforts of a gruelling and punishing season caught up

with us on a Wembley surface which always seemed to sap the energy from your whole body. Even before half-time my legs felt like lead weights and, when I looked around at my team-mates, pretty much everybody was in the same situation.

After the break QPR hit the bar, had two shots cleared off the line and we could barely stand up. If they'd scored they would certainly have gone on to win as there's no way we could have mustered a response. It's such a horrible feeling as a professional sportsman when your body is incapable of doing what your mind is telling it. But somehow we survived another 45 minutes purely on instinct and thankfully we were able to hold on as it would have been devastating to go through so much that season and end up empty-handed. Spurs were able to celebrate 100 years with a trophy which was nothing more than we deserved, although when I reflect on that campaign it still rankles that we didn't win the League. Given the ability and camaraderie in our squad we should have been good enough to win the old First Division.

It is one of my biggest regrets that we didn't manage it.

In the early eighties Aston Villa and Nottingham Forest both proved that Liverpool could be beaten over the course of a season, but our downfall was always consistency. Not so much against the big boys because we always fancied our chances against the best teams. However, we would always slip up against the sides in the bottom half of the table and the ones fighting relegation. We just didn't have the mental strength to swat the small teams aside like Liverpool did and I think we lacked a ruthless streak.

Our midfield was bursting with skill with the likes of Glenn, Ossie, Ricky, Tony and Micky Hazard, but I think it was lacking a nasty piece of work. I played quite a lot in the middle of the park and could hold my own although I'm certain if we'd had someone like Roy Keane, Patrick Vieira or Graeme Souness then we would have been the complete package. Those are the types of player you can count on when you have to go to St James' Park or Villa Park in mid-winter when it's freezing and pissing down with rain.

It was in games like that when we didn't see it through. We became known as the nearly team and that's not a moniker that sits well with me.

4

EUROPEAN GLORY

The chance to play European football was one of the biggest factors in my decision to join Spurs rather than West Brom. The make-up of the Spurs side was perfectly suited to playing against continental opposition and we had come agonisingly close to leaving our imprint on Europe before we struck gold in the 1984 UEFA Cup.

My first taste of playing competitively abroad came in the 1981/82 Cup Winner's Cup when we were paired with Ajax in the first round of the tournament. Ajax proved themselves to be the best club side in Europe throughout the eighties, but we totally destroyed them over two legs, thrashing them 3-1 in Amsterdam and then winning 3-0 in the home leg at the Lane. It was that victory, particularly the manner of it, which opened my eyes to the realistic possibility of success for Spurs at the highest level.

That season we reached the semi-final of the Cup Winner's Cup where we came up against the competition favourites, Barcelona. The final was to be staged at the Nou Camp that year so they had an added incentive to get past us. The first leg was at White Hart Lane and it will live long in my memory as the dirtiest and most violent match I've ever been involved in. There are not many, if any, more respected teams in Europe than Barcelona, but the thugs who masqueraded as players dragged the club into the gutter that evening.

From the first minute until the last they made it clear they were not interested in trying to play the free-flowing football which has become synonymous with Barca over the years. Instead they waged a dirty-tricks campaign against us and attempted to con the referee at every opportunity. If they weren't pulling the hairs on the back of your legs, elbowing you in the ribs when the ball wasn't there or dragging their studs down your Achilles then they would blatantly spit in your face as they ran past you.

Spitting is the lowest of the low in my book and it is extremely difficult, and arguably impossible, not to react when you are on the receiving end. Yet, while the antics of Barcelona were revolting, the most disappointing aspect of the whole episode was that we allowed ourselves to get caught up in it. It was sheer naivety on our part at this level and it would cost us the chance to play in a European Final. The only good to come out of it was that we learned a valuable and important lesson that would stand us in good stead for the future.

The referee was hopeless and while he red-carded one Barca player he should have sent off at least half a dozen of them. Their manager Udo Lattek was just as culpable as he spent the entire 90 minutes on the touchline yelling at his players to get stuck in.

The match looked certain to end scoreless until Ray Clemence threw an Olmo shot into his own net in the second half to give Barca the precious away goal. I popped up in the dying minutes to crash home a late consolation, but I still had a feeling it wouldn't be enough. Sadly I was proved right as Allan Simonsen scored the only goal of the game in Spain to send us spinning out of the tournament at the penultimate hurdle.

The following year we were back in the same competition after winning the FA Cup for the second time in 12 months. This time we didn't last long as we came up against Bayern Munich in the second round and were comprehensively outplayed as the Germans strolled through 5-1 on aggregate. It was another valuable lesson although this Spurs team were quick learners as the 1983/84 season would prove. This time we were in the UEFA Cup and with two valuable years' experience under our belts we felt capable of mounting a strong challenge. Guys like Glenn Hoddle, Ricky Villa and Ossie Ardiles were all tailor-made for this type of competition and when you have so many match winners in the team it allows the rest of the guys to play with a sense of freedom.

In the first round we were pitched in against a top-class Feyenoord side, who had Johann Cruyff and a youngster called Ruud Gullit in their ranks.

However, the Dutch masters didn't get much of a look in as Spurs produced the most mesmerising 45 minutes of football I've ever witnessed. We were 4-0 up at the break with Glenn at his magnificent best. He strutted around like a peacock that night as Gullit chased shadows. I genuinely believed we were quite capable of reaching double figures in the second half because Feyenoord surely must have been totally demoralised. Unfortunately I hadn't bargained on the genius of Cruyff. Not only was he one of the best players ever to grace the beautiful game but he also had the heart of a lion. Almost single-handedly he dragged his team back into the tie as Feyenoord staged a mini-comeback and we only ended up winning 4-2.

The press slated us the following day for taking our foot off the gas and I suppose some of it was deserved as we all thought the hard work had been done in the first period. Still, we didn't panic and when Tony Galvin scored an early goal in Rotterdam there was no way back for the Dutch. We won 2-0 on the night, but there was hardly a mention of the game in the newspapers the next day.

Sadly, hooliganism had reared its ugly head in Holland and some of the scenes I witnessed left me feeling sick to the pit of my stomach. Normally you're not aware of what's happening on the terraces when you are playing, but because we were 6-2 ahead on aggregate and the last third of the game was played out at a snail's pace, I could see all the fighting going on.

The problems arose because Feyenoord hadn't got rid of all their tickets and started selling them to English fans on the day of the game. They didn't bother to enforce any segregation so it was a recipe for disaster. To make matters worse there was a civil service strike in Rotterdam that day and the police resources were stretched to the limit. The troublemakers were virtually given carte blanche to run riot and they did just that.

Before the game there was a nasty atmosphere in the stadium and during the warm-up I witnessed several skirmishes. Spurs always used to carry a huge travelling support and there must have been 8,000 fans in the ground. There had been a couple of fights at White Hart Lane during the first leg and all the players were worried something like this would happen. Sure enough, it kicked off big-style and I can still remember walking off the pitch at the end of the game and seeing people getting smashed in the face with bottles and bricks. The whole thing overshadowed another great Spurs performance and that was a pity because we deserved a lot of credit after taking some fearful stick following the first leg. After the match I swapped shirts with Gullit and to this day it still takes pride of place in my ex-wife's loft!

Next up was Bayern Munich, who had ended our Euro dreams the previous season in pretty spectacular fashion. Having been hammered 4-1 in the Olympic Stadium 12 months earlier we were pleased to bring them back to London with just a one-goal deficit. Michael Rummenigge scored a last-minute goal and while they thought that would be enough, we considered 1-0 a good result.

I don't think I've ever been so happy to reach the sanctuary of the dressing room after a match because the conditions were the coldest I experienced as a player. It was minus 12 in Munich and because it was so cold we started our warm-up under the stadium. I had worked up a decent sweat as I wanted to make sure I didn't pull a muscle. However, I remember running out on to the park and the beads of sweat on my brow turned instantly to ice. It was freezing beyond belief although the result lifted our spirits and we were confident of turning them over and gaining our revenge at White Hart Lane.

Thankfully, the temperature was the right side of zero for the return in North London. It was a frustrating game and for 75 minutes we just couldn't find a way through a stubborn

Bayern defence. They were rock solid at the back and they were always dangerous on the counter attack so we really had to be on our toes. We were fortunate to escape with our goal still intact when they caught us on the counter as we piled forward in search of an equaliser. Then, just when our cause appeared forlorn, we profited from a great piece of good fortune.

Glenn was the orchestrator, floating in a free-kick to the back post which I headed into the path of Steve Archibald. He looked at least a yard offside, but the linesman kept his flag down and Archie crashed home from close range to level the tie. Suddenly, the pressure was on the Germans and it was such a terrific feeling to see them crack.

Once again Glenn was our creative spark, with a perfectly weighted long ball into the path of Mark Falco. Mark was strong as an ox and, after holding off the challenge of the Bayern defender, he nonchalantly slotted the ball into the net to earn us a place in the last eight.

We'd overcome a massive hurdle by beating the favourites and a team who wiped the floor with us the previous year. We were brimming with confidence and I wasn't bothered who we got in the quarter-final draw. I considered Spurs to be the best side left in the competition and I didn't fear anybody after conquering Bayern Munich.

Our next opponents were Austria Vienna and while we beat them 2-0 at home the victory came at a price. Glenn had been struggling for a while with an ankle injury and he never played again that season after aggravating it against the Austrians.

It was a real niggly affair and I had a few run-ins with their captain, Robert Sara. He'd caught me late with a couple of snide tackles and I'd just about had enough. I told him if he did it again he'd regret it. Sure enough, he left his studs in the next time we went for the ball and laughed as he walked away. I bided my time and when he went for a ball on the touchline I sprinted 40 yards to hit him. I made sure I got the ball first, but I went right through him and he hit the ground like a ton of bricks. The ref never even awarded a foul which I found quite amusing. Sara's complaints fell on deaf ears and he kept telling me I was off my head and that I would pay for my actions in the second leg.

The Barcelona game had taught me to meet fire with fire because if foreign teams think you are weak then they'll try to exploit you at every opportunity. Of course, you had to be careful not to overstep the mark because there was no point getting yourself needlessly sent off. That was the case in Vienna when the Austrians tried everything they could to provoke me, but I wasn't falling into their trap. We took the lead over there through Alan Brazil and his early goal put the tie well beyond their reach. They just lost the plot after that although we refused to become embroiled in any feuds. I was covered in bruises at the end of the game, but it was worth it as there was no way I wanted to miss the semi-final. Ossie nabbed a late equaliser to make it 2-2 on the night and now only Hadjuk Split stood between us and a place in the UEFA Cup Final.

Our away form had been terrific in Europe although we let ourselves down in the former Yugoslavia in the first leg of our semi-final. Mark Falco had given us the lead when he scored from a rebound after the Hadjuk keeper saved his penalty. We were in total control and cruising, only to switch off in the closing minutes of the match allowing them to score twice. It was a real boot in the balls for us and the only consolation was that we'd at least managed to secure an away goal. And what a priceless one it would turn out to be.

At White Hart Lane Micky Hazard proved himself to be an able deputy for Glenn Hoddle when he settled our nerves with a well executed free-kick. He spotted a gap in their defensive wall and as they jumped when he went to hit the ball, Micky fired it under them and into the bottom corner of the net. In the celebrations that followed Micky lost his contact lens and was fumbling around the centre spot trying to find it when somebody stood on it and wrecked it.

The previous year Keith made the entire squad get their eyes tested. He arranged for an optician to come to the ground and the results of the tests were incredible. Only a third of the team had perfect vision so Keith ordered the rest of us, including myself, to wear contact lenses when we played matches. And what a difference it made. In the first game when we all wore them we thrashed Birmingham 5-0! I've worn them ever since and I sometimes wonder how I managed to play for almost twenty years without them when my eyesight was so poor.

Micky had to go off to find a replacement lens, but he was back on the pitch in time for the amazing celebrations at the final whistle. His goal had ensured we would be facing Anderlecht, who beat Nottingham Forest in the other semi, in the UEFA Cup Final. It all seemed so surreal and things seemed to be happening so fast for someone who was playing non-league football only three years before.

The manager had played such a huge part in our success

and on a personal level I owed him so much. Keith had shown real faith in me by pitching me into the team when I was an unknown rookie. He was so popular amongst the players and while I've been in a lot of dressing rooms where people barely tolerated the boss, our affection for the gaffer was one hundred per cent genuine.

That's why it came as such a bombshell when he announced he was going to quit the club at the end of the season. His decision was like a bolt from the blue and I was devastated. The chairman, Irving Scholar, wanted to adopt a more hands-on approach and was keen to restructure the way the club was run. Irving wanted to have the final say on what players were bought and sold and, under the new remit, Keith would only be responsible for coaching. He knew the gaffer would never accept that in a million years and in my opinion it was just a ploy to get him out.

Keith had run the club from top to bottom for the best part of a decade and his methods had brought Spurs a great deal of success. It was Irving's prerogative as he owned the club, but I think he resented Keith's influence around White Hart Lane. Keith was an old-school Yorkshireman and he was far too proud and too stubborn to let anyone else have a say on team affairs. That was his domain and if he couldn't have total control then he was offski. All the lads were determined to win the UEFA Cup for him because that would be the best leaving present possible.

We were so fired up ahead of the first leg in Belgium until a tragic incident at our hotel the night before the game took the wind right out of our sails. I remember lying in bed when I heard a massive bang outside my window. I thought it was a car exhaust misfiring or a firework going off. The following morning at breakfast Keith told us that a young Spurs fan had been shot while drinking in the bar underneath our hotel. All the lads just felt numb and it was difficult to try and focus on a football match after you've just been told one of our supporters had lost his life.

The match was pretty much a blur for me and it felt like I was on autopilot. It was a weird experience, but we still had a cup final to win regardless of what had happened. Paul Miller gave us the lead at the start of the second half and we were good value to take a lead back to the Lane. However, Anderlecht caught us out with a late sucker punch when the Danish international Morten Olsen bundled the ball home following a goalmouth scramble. Under the circumstances 1-1 was a good result although we suffered a blow late in the game when our skipper, Steve Perryman, picked up a yellow card which ruled him out of the second leg. Everybody was gutted for Stevie as he was an inspirational leader and he'd been an integral part of the club's recent success.

I must confess to mixed emotions when Keith took me aside after the game and told me I would be leading out the team at White Hart Lane in Stevie's absence although my over-riding feeling was of enormous pride. Stevie was still the club captain and he would play a vital role in the build-up to the second leg.

ITV had paid a fortune to secure the television rights for the final and part of the deal we had at the time was that a slice of any TV revenue went into the players' pool. But the chairman was having none of it. Stevie went to see Irving and asked for the £100,000 the players felt they were entitled to.

Irving, like Keith, was a stubborn bugger and the more we made an issue of it the more determined he was to dig his heels in. Keith said he backed us to the hilt so Stevie went back to see the chairman and told him the players were going on strike if an agreement couldn't be reached. Irving was furious and decided to call our bluff. 'If they don't want to play in a UEFA Cup Final then I'll play the youth team,' he declared.

We continued to train, hoping the matter would be resolved, but we refused to go to the team hotel on the Monday night ahead of the game on Wednesday. We didn't go to the hotel on the Tuesday night either and by this stage Keith was starting to get really worried. He was pleading with us to forget about the bonus money although, come the day of the game, both the players and the chairman were sticking to their guns.

It wasn't really about money as each player would only have got about £8,000. It was a point of principle as we all felt the chairman was taking liberties and had shafted us. We all stuck together and at lunchtime our solidarity was rewarded. We received a message from the chairman saying he had agreed to pay us a percentage of the money from ITV. I'm pretty sure we would have played anyway, but it was a nice feeling to get one over on Irving and the boys were pretty pleased with themselves.

That was the first battle won. Now we had to get ourselves mentally attuned to take on Anderlecht without a host of our star names. We were missing Glenn, Stevie, Ricky Villa, Garth Crooks and Ossie was only fit enough to be on the bench. The gaffer also opted to go with Tony Parks in goal rather than Ray Clemence. Tony had replaced Clem a few weeks earlier when he picked up an injury and had done exceptionally well. Most of the lads thought Clem would be back in for the final as he was an established England international at the time and he was one of the key members of our squad. Keith felt Tony deserved to keep the number one jersey and a distraught Ray Clemence missed out. White Hart Lane was half-full three hours before kick-off at 5pm and I've never known an atmosphere like it. The place was jumping and I felt an enormous surge of adrenalin when the team coach rolled up at the stadium.

A nil-nil draw would have been good enough for us to emerge victorious and that's the way it looked until Morten Olsen took a hand in the matter on the hour mark. He played a sublime defence-splitting pass to set up Pavel Czernatynski, who calmly slotted the ball past Parksy. Anderlecht were a top-class team and, as defending champions, they were not intimidated by 52,000 Spurs fans baying for their blood.

Chelsea's director of football, Frank Arnesen, was in their team that night and he was actually replaced by Eidur Gudjohnsen's dad Arnor midway through the second half. The gaffer threw on Ossie and Ally Dick as we desperately searched for an equaliser, but their goal had knocked the stuffing out of us and it just wasn't happening. We weren't creating any chances and the Belgians looked on course to win consecutive UEFA Cup Finals.

Thankfully, fate intervened with six minutes remaining as I experienced the most exhilarating moment of my life. Micky curled in a free kick from the right and it caused complete panic in the Anderlecht defence. It was bouncing all over the place when Ossie took a huge swipe at it from no more than two yards. He couldn't miss, but somehow it crashed off the crossbar and they booted it clear. I think they started to relax then, only for Micky to whip the ball back into the danger area. His cross was intended for Mark Falco, but the defender pushed him out of the way as he went to head it.

Suddenly the ball hit my chest on the edge of the box and after taking a touch I found myself six yards from goal. Morten Olsen had tried to tackle me but amidst all the mayhem I somehow found the strength to hold off his challenge and slot home the equaliser. I didn't panic and I think my days playing as a striker for Weymouth and Porstmouth when I was younger stood me in good stead. The crowd went berserk and it is almost impossible to describe the elation I felt when the ball hit the back of the net. Put it this way, when Mick Fitzgerald won the Grand National on Rough Quest and said it was better than sex, I knew, if you will pardon the pun, exactly where he was coming from! It was the best moment of my entire career although at that particular moment I didn't get much time to enjoy it because we still had a European trophy to win.

My equaliser forced the match into extra-time although the additional 30 minutes were pretty dire with both teams reluctant to commit men forward for fear of being caught on the counter attack. Almost inevitably, the match would be decided on penalties.

As captain I felt obliged to lead by example and nominated myself to take the first kick in the shoot-out. I wasn't nervous when I walked up to take it. I was in the zone and I'd made up my mind to smash it into the top left-hand corner. I executed it perfectly to give us an early advantage and when the ball hit the net there was a huge sense of relief. Nobody wants to be remembered as the player who cost their team the chance of a major victory by missing a penalty.

After Parksy had saved the Belgians' opening effort, Mark Falco, Steve Archibald and Gary Stevens had set it up for Danny Thomas to claim the glory. My heart sank when he missed it and while all the lads were consoling him I gave him a slap around the head and called him a silly c***. Thankfully, Parksy spared his blushes, saving Arnor Gudjohnsen's penalty to spark incredible scenes of joy at White Hart Lane. I don't think it gets any better than winning a European trophy on your own ground, in front of your own supporters. I was overcome with emotion at the end and I remember running to Keith when it was all over. He'd been like a father figure to me since I joined Spurs and I was just as pleased for him as I was for myself.

We both agreed that Stevie should collect the cup, but the skipper was having none of it. He turned to me and said: 'You're the captain tonight, Graham, and you did more than anybody else on the pitch to win us the cup so I'll just watch if you don't mind.' I appreciated that.

The trophy weighed a ton and I barely had enough energy left to lift it above my head. It was after 11pm when the game finished and the players were still on the pitch celebrating beyond midnight. The 1984 UEFA Cup Final is the match Spurs fans most remember me for. I'm happy with that because I think it was the best game of football I ever played.

5

WHO PUT CHARLIE IN THE STAND?

Within 48 hours of Spurs winning the UEFA Cup Keith Burkinshaw had walked out on the club. As far as I was concerned the chairman, Irving Scholar, should never have allowed that to happen. I had a lot of time for Irving and he'd looked after me financially during my time at White Hart Lane. If you did well at Spurs and gave 100 per cent effort and commitment then the chairman would make sure you were well rewarded. If he thought you were slacking then you'd be out the door before your feet could touch the ground.

Irving appreciated hard workers which made it even more difficult to understand why he got rid of Keith. The gaffer was a legendary figure at the club and he was universally popular with everyone at Spurs, apart from Irving, who appeared to resent his power base, and Steve Archibald. However, that was hardly surprising as Archie didn't really like anybody but himself. I actually got on great with him although I knew how to take him.

Keith and Archie fell out a couple of times and hardly ever spoke to each other. Steve was always demanding to be in the starting line-up every week and if he was ever dropped or substituted he would demand to be sold to a club who would appreciate him more. There's no way Archie could survive at any of the top clubs today where there is squad rotation amongst the strikers.

Archie thought he was the bee's knees and while there's no doubt he was a terrific player and a great goalscorer, he'd have you believe he was better than Pele. He was an arrogant c***. That's the best way of describing him because it was always me, me, me with Archie. As I mentioned before, I actually got on fine with him and he was really good with me when I signed for Spurs, but Keith didn't like his selfish attitude and that's why there was always going to be conflict.

I remember one match against Leicester when Archie picked up an injury and kept shouting to the bench that he wanted to come off. There was only one substitute at the time and because we'd already used ours Keith wanted Archie to stay on the pitch. Archie refused and claimed there was no way he could play on and risk further aggravating his knee. Two days later he turned up for training as if nothing had happened and the gaffer went ballistic, accusing him of feigning injury and letting his team-mates down.

There were no airs and graces with Keith, a typically blunt Yorkshireman, who was straight as a dye. What you saw was what you got and he was never one to shirk from making big decisions, regardless of how unpopular it would make him. There were plenty of occasions when players disagreed with him although because he never had any favourites I think everybody respected him.

Filling his shoes was always going to be a monumental job and I'm not sure Peter Shreeve was quite up to it. Peter had been part of the backroom staff and as a coach he had few peers. His knowledge of the game was encyclopedic, but I've always maintained he was a much better assistant than a manager. Also, he was taking charge just days after the club had achieved one of the greatest moments in its history so he was on a hiding to nothing really.

Peter was always one of the lads and had been close to most of the players. Now he had to distance himself and he found that aspect tough to deal with. The main positive for him was that he didn't have to change things. We already had a strong squad in place so there was no need to spend fortunes in the transfer market. His philosophies were the same as Keith's when it came to playing attractive, free-flowing football and we went close to winning the championship during his first season in charge. But, once again, we came up agonisingly short and after challenging hard for three quarters of the campaign, we couldn't maintain our effort until May.

We eventually finished third, but it was downhill all the way for me at Spurs after that. There were rumours about his departure from as early October following a poor start and a shock League Cup defeat at the hands of Portsmouth. We were struggling in the league and I think as time went on Peter lost both the plot and the dressing room. He stripped me of the captaincy and gave it to Ray Clemence. He claimed the pressure and the responsibility of the position were affecting my performances. That was bullshit because, if anything, I was Spurs' best player that season. I think Peter was just clutching at straws by that stage and it came as no surprise when he was relieved of his duties at the end of the season.

Things had ended badly under Peter but they were about to get ten times worse when David Pleat took over in the summer of 1986. Right from our first meeting he made it clear I wasn't going to be part of his plans. This was after he telephoned me when he got the job to say how much he looked forward to working with me. Typical Pleat. A two-faced wanker. When our paths crossed at the start of pre-season training he informed me that I wasn't his type of player and the first thing he would be doing was signing a centre-half. Charming.

Richard Gough was bought as my replacement with Spurs pipping Rangers to his signature. They paid £750,000 for him, which was a huge amount of money back then. Rangers were desperate to sign him but he had to move to England as Dundee United refused to sell him to another Scottish club.

Gough's arrival only made me determined to stick two fingers up at Pleat and prove that I was a much better player than he gave me credit for. As it turned out, he couldn't get me out of the team. I moved into midfield to accommodate Goughie and Gary Mabbutt, but I was playing so well he couldn't drop me. He realised it would have been to the detriment of the side if I didn't play so through gritted teeth he had to name me in the starting line-up every week before I eventually got my move to Rangers.

I was distraught to leave Spurs because I'd grown to love the club and the amazing fans. However, as I couldn't stand the sight of the manager I felt it was better for all concerned if I moved on. At least I was heading off to Scotland with a host of memories to cherish plus two FA Cup winner's medals and a UEFA Cup winner's medal in my pocket.

Those triumphs were the highlights of my seven-year stint at the Lane although the incident most of the supporters remember me for came in a North London derby at Highbury on New Year's Day 1986. The game itself was pretty much a non-event mainly due to the conditions. Parts of the pitch were rock solid with frost as Arsenal's undersoil heating hadn't worked properly and there were big white patches all over the pitch. It was almost impossible to keep your footing and, as a result, there wasn't much decent football played.

At one point the referee was going to abandon the match although both teams said they were quite happy to continue. Nothing much happened until just after half-time when Arsenal cleared one of our corners and quickly played the ball out to Charlie Nicholas. I spotted the danger and rushed back hoping to make an interception, but Charlie got to the pass just in front of me. I was travelling at a fair rate of knots and as the pitch was pretty slippy there was no way I was for stopping. If I couldn't get the ball then I was going to make sure I got the man. I raised my elbow and clattered into Charlie who went sprawling over a metal railing and into the crowd. It was a shocking challenge and there would have been no complaints if the referee had shown me a red card. Normally I was always hard but fair. This was brutal and unfair.

Thankfully, Charlie was OK because he could have really suffered a serious injury. As he was flying into the Highbury main stand, my momentum had taken me careering into the Arsenal dug-out. There were bodies everywhere and I remember their physio asking me if I was alright as I was on my hands and knees. 'I'm fine thanks,' I said. 'Well you're not now,' he replied, before decking me with a right hook. The cheeky bastard connected right on my nose and there was blood everywhere.

All hell then broke loose as the two benches became embroiled in a mini riot while the Arsenal fans were baying for even more of my blood. It was mayhem and when it all calmed down I was the only one to get booked. And every game after that the Spurs fans used to chant: 'Who put Charlie in the stand? Robbo, Robbo!' During the UEFA Cup clash with Steaua Bucharest last season, I made a half-time appearance on the pitch and they started singing it again. It was fantastic to hear it after so many years.

I used to relish those North London derbies because there was no quarter asked or given and the passion of the supporters was incredible. They were totally different to an Old Firm match because the atmosphere at Ibrox or Parkhead is generated mainly through hatred. After a Spurs v Arsenal match you can go back to most pubs and you will find the two sets of supporters having a drink together. They despise each other for 90 minutes and then, for a lot of them, it's all forgotten about. You don't get an awful lot of that with Rangers and Celtic. In fact I don't know any boozers in Glasgow where both lots of fans will go after the game to have a drink together. That just doesn't happen.

6

DEATH DEFYING PATRIOT GAMES

My first England call-up came at the end of my second full season with Spurs and as someone who has always been patriotic it was such a proud moment. Spurs were on a summer tour to Trinidad and Tobago when Keith pulled me and Glenn Hoddle aside and told us we had been called into the England set-up for the Home Internationals. The West Indies trip was just a jolly really and we spent most of the time playing golf and getting pissed. I was actually in the bar having a few beers when Keith broke the good news so it was only right to order up another few as a means of celebration.

I flew home early and joined up with the rest of the squad at Bisham Abbey in High Wycombe. I was nervous as hell when I walked into the team hotel and glanced around at players like Terry Butcher, Bryan Robson, Ray Wilkins, Kenny Samson and Peter Shilton. I'm glad Glenn was there because he knew all of them already and he helped break the ice by making the introductions. Glenn had been a great mate since I joined Spurs and as we lived close to each other in North London we adopted the same pub as our local. He was also my room-mate on that first trip and his presence certainly made me feel more at ease.

To be perfectly honest I was convinced I'd been brought into the squad purely to give me a taste of what to expect if I kept performing at a high level for Spurs. However, on the Thursday, two days before our first game with Northern Ireland in Belfast, Bobby Robson told me I would be in the starting line-up.

Don Howe was the defensive coach with England at the time and he really knew his stuff. Don was one of the best coaches of the last 50 years and he spent hours and hours with me going over tactics, set-plays and my responsibilities. After a few days working with Don I felt like Franz Beckenbauer although I played more like Frank Spencer in the opening 15 minutes at Windsor Park.

Terry Butcher was my central defensive partner and while I consider myself to be a true patriot, I don't think anyone comes close to touching Big Butch when it comes to a love for your country. The gusto with which he belted out the national anthem before kick-off made the hairs on the back of my neck stand up and it was at that moment I truly realised what playing for England was all about. It's the ultimate honour and after being inspired by Terry's stirring rendition of 'God Save the Queen' I was determined not to let anybody down. I find it staggering he's now assistant manager with the Scottish national team.

But, if anything, I tried too hard at the start of the game and I almost got my international career off to the worst possible start by putting the ball through my own net. Noel Brotherston played a ball in from the flank and it arrived at that awkward height for a defender when you don't know whether to head it or boot it clear. I was caught in two minds and didn't have a clue what to do. I was facing my own goal and in the end I opted to try and head it over the crossbar. However, just at the last second it dipped right in front of me and I didn't catch it properly. It was heading right into the bottom corner and I would have looked a complete idiot if Peter Shilton hadn't pulled off a world-class save to spare my blushes. Cheers Shilts! The game ended scoreless and was pretty much a non-event, but I was delighted not to lose on my debut and to come away with a clean sheet.

Scotland were next up at Wembley on the Wednesday night and again I didn't expect to start because I didn't do anything out of the ordinary and I thought Bobby might want to give Alvin Martin or Russell Osman a run out in central defence. To my surprise Bobby came up to me on the Tuesday and said: 'You did well on Saturday so I'm going to give you another go, son.' That's all the manager said to me, yet, delivered at the right time, one sentence of encouragement can work wonders for your self-belief. Suddenly I felt as if I belonged in the England team and I had a blinder against Scotland the following night.

The game always sticks in my head because it was the day of the Derby and my Spurs team-mate Alan Brazil, who was in the Scotland squad, had given me a massive tip for Teenoso. Alan had backed it ante-post at 33-1 and when Scotland manager Jock Stein found out, he wanted a piece of the action. Teenoso went off the 9-2 favourite but Big Jock told Alan that if he wanted to start against England then he better get him 20-1. Alan told him to get stuffed and when he also refused to give him 10-1, Jock told him to forget about playing.

Under a magnificent Lester Piggot ride, Teenoso romped

home much to the delight of the entire Scotland and England teams, who had both steamed in thanks to Alan Brazil. I'm not sure if Alan was too bothered about being involved because I got the impression he preferred getting pissed to playing. He was someone who lived life to the full and he was always terrific company.

If he had been playing, I'd have definitely booted him off the park. But as he wasn't, I reserved that treatment for Charlie Nicholas. Charlie was the best thing since sliced bread at that time north of the border and about 70,000 Scots had descended on Wembley to see him put the big bad English to the sword. The Tartan Army were out in force that night and I couldn't quite believe how so many Scotland fans managed to get tickets for an England home match. When I ran onto the pitch at the start of the game I struggled to see any England fans although that helped fire me up even more. The only thing on my mind that night was to silence the Jocks and I took great satisfaction when we dished out a footballing lesson. The final score was only 2-0, courtesy of goals from Bryan Robson and Gordon Cowans, but we battered Scotland from start to finish.

I actually watched the game on ESPN recently and I couldn't believe the ferocity of the tackles that were flying in. There was nothing 'friendly' about England v Scotland matches and it's a shame they scrapped the Home Internationals. Those games really got the blood boiling and it would be great if they could find a space in the calendar to bring them back because I know the players relished the Battle of Britain encounters. For Scotland fans it didn't get any better than beating England and that's why the games always had an edge.

The following summer we played Scotland at Hampden and it was like walking into the lion's den. The atmosphere in Glasgow was sensational and if you can't perform in an arena like that as a footballer then you should be looking for another career. Again I was taken aback when Bobby named me in the starting line-up because I only joined up with the squad 24 hours before the match as I'd been involved in Spurs' UEFA Cup Final win on the Thursday night. I'd also been partying all night and hadn't been to my bed when I caught the first shuttle from Heathrow to Glasgow along with Micky Hazard. We got a taxi to the Marine Hotel in Troon where the team were based and the gaffer told us to take it easy in training as he knew we'd had such a tough game the previous night. Reading between the lines I took it that neither me or Micky would be starting so when Bryan Robson and Ray Wilkins knocked on my door after dinner to take me out for a few celebratory beers, I thought a refusal might offend. It sounds incredible now, but nobody thought much of going on the piss just hours before such an important game.

I was still tanked up from the night before and when I woke up on Saturday morning I felt horrific. However, I quickly sobered up when the gaffer told me I was in the side to face Scotland. Micky, who was in the squad for the first time, was named among the substitutes although Bobby told him he would definitely get on at some stage. I'd been hugely impressed by Micky since coming to Spurs and I honestly felt he possessed as much skill as Glenn Hoddle. He was also a fantastic athlete and when we used to do cross-country runs in training he would be miles ahead of everybody else.

Unfortunately, Micky's downfalls were injuries and

hamburgers. I've never seen anybody who could devour so many McDonald's at one sitting. Micky would easily demolish five burgers and then go next door for a helping of fish and chips. Throughout his career he suffered from tight hamstrings and he always needed to spend a huge amount of time warming-up.

The first half didn't go well for us and Scotland were leading 1-0 at half-time. Bobby told us he would give it another ten minutes before making some changes. When we equalised through Tony Woodcock at the start of the second half, the gaffer sent Micky to warm-up behind our goals with a view to putting him on. But Bobby made one change, then another one, and then a third one. All this time, Micky was still running up and down behind the goal. The final whistle went and Bobby was going through his post-match talk in the dressing room when Micky walked in. He looked at him and said: 'Oh shit. I'm really sorry, Micky. I completely forgot all about you.' Micky was crestfallen because he'd spent 80 minutes warming up for nothing and he was the only one who didn't see the funny side.

We played Russia a few days later and then went to South America but Keith Burkinshaw had called up Bobby Robson and asked him if he could release any Spurs players who were unlikely to be involved as they were going on a tour of Swaziland. Poor Micky was allowed to leave and his departure signaled the end of his involvement with the national team. Sadly, he would never win an England cap and that was a travesty for someone of his ability.

I remember during that same get-together we were working on shooting practice with John Barnes crossing balls into the penalty box for the strikers. Bobby went through the drill about four times and on every occasion the forwards failed to get on the end of it. He was going crazy but he couldn't give the player in question a bollocking because he couldn't remember his name. The gaffer then turned to Ray Wilkins and asked him what the big black lad was called. 'Bluther,' replied Ray.

'For fuck sake, Bluther, when are you going to get on the end of a fucking cross?' blasted Bobby, much to the amusement of the lads who were rolling about the ground laughing. Luther Blissett took it in good spirits and from that day onwards he was affectionately known as Bluther.

There was never a dull moment when Bobby was around and I remember his tactics briefing before we played Hungary in a European Cup qualifier. He named his team when we were having lunch and then proceeded to go through the set-piece formations.

'Hoddle, when we get a throw-in I'd like you to take it,' Bobby said as he glanced around the room. 'When we get a corner, Hoddle I'd like you to take that as well,' he added. 'If we get a free-kick or a penalty, can you take them as well please, Hoddle,' Bobby went on. Just at that Kenny Sansom stood up and said, 'No offence gaffer, but the rest of us might as well stay in the hotel tonight.' As it turned out the last laugh was on us with Glenn scoring the winner against Hungary with a stunning free-kick.

After drawing with Scotland at Hampden we hosted Russia at Wembley before flying out on our tour of South America. We totally under-estimated the Russians and on a blistering hot afternoon they passed us off the pitch. Mike Duxbury from Man United trod on the ball to gift them a lead and it was downhill all the way after that. The visitors ran out comfortable 2-0 winners and I remember the crowd booing us off the park at the end of the match.

As we sat in the dressing room we could hear the calls for Bobby to be sacked and it was pretty uncomfortable to be honest. It was totally over the top as we'd only lost a friendly, but it was a similar story in the newspapers the following morning. The majority of the red tops were demanding Bobby's head and I recall reading the obituaries when we were on the flight to Brazil on the Monday morning.

I was a major doubt for the trip as I'd picked up a groin injury, but with Terry Butcher ruled out, Bobby was keen for me to travel. When we arrived in Rio I could still feel a small twinge in my groin so I was told do some running work with the physio on my own while the rest of the lads trained. The manager said he would leave me out of the Brazil game, but if my injury responded to treatment then I would be back in the side against Uruguay.

I found it a bit strange that Fred Street, the England physio at the time, wanted me to do 200-metre sprints, given the nature of my injury. I just got on with it though, and at first I felt fine as I ran around the perimeter of Flamenco's ground in 100-degree heat. I'd done a couple of laps when I had to rush off to the toilet with horrific stomach pains. I had diarrhoea and was violently sick and I was still there ten minutes later when Fred came in looking for me. After he'd thrown some cold water over me I felt a little better, but when I walked back onto the pitch I doubled over in agony again and almost collapsed.

Realising something wasn't right, Fred got me back to the hotel as quickly as possible and arranged for the team doctor to examine me. I could see the panic in his face as he called for a second opinion and within half an hour I was lying on the surgeon's table. My appendix had ruptured and the doc told me that if I hadn't been diagnosed immediately then I'd probably have been dead within the hour. I was in so much pain by this stage I didn't have a clue what was going on until I woke up the following morning after my operation.

Fred's and the doc's quick thinking had saved my life although I still felt as if I was dying when I opened my eyes. In a scene straight out of a horror movie I was lying on a musty smelling bed in the most disgusting hospital imaginable covered from head to toe in blood. I was all alone in a tiny room no bigger than a broom cupboard and I was completely confused. The surgeon had obviously carried out the operation but nobody had cleaned me up afterwards. I didn't know where I was and I started to panic. When I began shouting and screaming, the nurses ran into my room although they didn't speak any English and didn't have a clue what I was saying. They did eventually wash me and bring me a clean gown to wear and then Ray Wilkins, Bryan Robson, the gaffer and Fred came in to see me. I was so relieved to see some familiar faces although they could only stay for a little while as they were playing Brazil that night.

Indeed, while Mark Hateley and John Barnes were putting the mighty Brazilians to the sword in the Maracana, I was lying in a fleapit hospital so weak I couldn't move a muscle. On one hand I was so delighted to be alive, yet on the other I couldn't comprehend the state of the place England had put me in and the butcher's job that had been carried out on my stomach. The surgeon's procedure must have been as subtle as one of my tackles because, even to this day, I still have a huge scar and a massive indent just above my waist.

My spell in Rio was a living nightmare and, to make matters worse, none of the England officials who were part of the tour could be bothered to come and visit me. Kenny Sansom, Gary Stevens, Tony Woodcock and Terry Fenwick all popped in to see me before they left for Uruguay, but after that I was on my own.

During those first two days in hospital I had nothing to eat and drink and I was becoming seriously dehydrated because the stifling heat was unbearable. Eventually I managed to make a phone call to my wife Ann and begged her to try and get me some help. She rang Keith Burkinshaw who was straight on the phone to the club chairman, Irving Scholar. The one thing about Spurs was they always looked after you, on and off the pitch, and within 24 hours Irving had sent a private nurse to Brazil. England heard about this and to say they were unhappy was an understatement. In an attempt to save face they told Dick Wragg from the FA to stay behind in Rio with me although their actions were nothing more than an after-thought.

I never understood why England didn't arrange medical assistance for me in the first place but the arrival of the nurse was a godsend. She was a proper Florence Nightingale and I don't know how I would have been able to cope without her. She could see I didn't have any energy so the first thing she did was go to get me loads of fresh fruit, biscuits and plenty to drink. The following day, when I finally had enough strength to move, she discharged me from hospital and checked me into a five-star hotel.

I was in a wheelchair for a few days and then I spent the next fortnight recuperating before I was allowed to fly back to England. I was so relieved to get back home – amazingly England paid for me to travel First Class! – although Ann hardly recognised me because I'd lost over two stone in weight because of my South American ordeal. If it hadn't been for Ann's help then I shudder to think what would have happened to me over there, however the FA didn't appreciate her inter-ference. They tried to dissuade Spurs from sending out a nurse but thankfully the club totally ignored them.

Despite playing the best football of my career when I recov-ered, I would never represent my country at full international level again. There were different occasions when Mark Wright, Terry Butcher, Dave Watson and Alvin Martin had all been unavailable, yet I still didn't get a look in. I don't blame Bobby Robson as I got the impression the decision had been taken out of his hands, but being shunned by England cut me to the core.

At one point, I was called into a squad of thirty for a match against East Germany the following season, which gave me a glimmer of hope. However, I was one of eight players released back to their clubs. My final game for England came when I was captain for a B international against New Zealand at the City Ground in 1984. It was as low key and instantly forget-table as it sounds. I knew then that my time had come and gone and it's one of my biggest regrets that I didn't get the opportunity to win more than six caps.

7

HARD AS NAILS

I'd never really been regarded as a hard man during the early days and it wasn't until I joined Spurs that I forged a reputation that would live with me for the rest of my career.

In my first North London derby against Arsenal I remember crunching into a tackle with Kenny Samson on the halfway line. The crowd loved it and in the newspapers a couple of days later there was an article branding me the new Dave Mackay. From that moment I became the hard man of the Spurs defence. The tag just stuck and being the type of character I am there was never any chance of me playing it down.

As a young player I quickly realised that you needed to be strong mentally as well as physically if you wanted to succeed. When I was an apprentice at Portsmouth I was boot boy for Steve Foster and a few of the senior players at Fratton Park. If they found even the tiniest speck of dirt on their boots then you would be taken into the gym and given a proper hiding. I only made that mistake once. And the experience toughened me up and taught me how to look after myself. It certainly didn't leave me scarred or anything like that because, even to this day, I still keep in contact with Steve. If something like that happened at any of the top clubs now there would be a full-scale police investigation and Steve would probably find himself behind bars. How times change.

Filling Dave Mackay's shoes was going to be a tall order as he was regarded as one of the best, and toughest, players in the history of Spurs. The picture of him grabbing Billy Bremner is one of the most famous images in sport and Dave is still revered at White Hart Lane. I knew he was a tough act to follow in every sense although never being one to shirk a challenge I was going to have a pretty good crack at it. Now that I was perceived as a hard man I was going to make sure I played up to that billing at every opportunity.

As a defender you need every possible advantage over your opponent so on the back of being bracketed in the tough guy category, I introduced intimidation into my game. It wasn't difficult as I always had an unflinching desire to win and was fiercely competitive. In some ways I was adopting a different persona when I went on the park to make me appear more of a threat to the players I would be marking.

I was always well built and strong in the tackle anyway so this new approach came easily. Jason Cundy always used to say I had the biggest calf muscles in the world. They were perfect for crunching into the back of strikers. I used to spend hours in the gym doing leg weights and that's why I rarely lost a 50/50 tackle. Tackling is an art form although sadly it's one that is being eroded from the game in the 21st century. You simply can't get away with the challenges I used to make which is a shame because football is supposed to be a contact sport.

After a couple of seasons with Spurs my reputation started to go before me. It's something that worked in my favour as there were plenty of strikers who were already in your pocket before a ball was kicked. It also helped that my central defensive partner, Paul Miller, was the type of guy you'd want beside you in the trenches. Maxi was a ferocious competitor and it was a pleasure to play alongside him for the best part of six seasons. We had a great understanding and I think it was even better than the one I formed with Terry Butcher at Rangers and, albeit briefly, with England.

I don't think Maxi ever got the credit he deserved. He was a real unsung hero, who played with his heart on his sleeve and never shirked a challenge in his life. During his spell in charge, Keith Burkinshaw kept strengthening the squad and everybody assumed Maxi would be the one to drop out when people like Gary Stevens, Gary Mabbutt, Paul Price and John Lacy arrived at the club. But, along with Chris Hughton and Steve Perryman, we had formed such a formidable back line that the manager found it impossible to leave any of us out. In the end Maxi got his just rewards as he was part of the hat-trick of cup final successes we enjoyed at the start of the eighties.

He was also a great intimidator and we used to love trying to frighten the life out of players before a ball was kicked. When we were walking out the tunnel we would tell them what was going to be in store for them. Just for good measure I would clatter them at the first opportunity and it's surprising how many players didn't have the stomach for a good battle. During the North London derbies I always felt I had the edge on Charlie Nicholas and Tony Woodcock. They were both terrific players, but I don't think they relished the mental or physical battles.

If it came down purely to skill then it was no contest although I'm a firm believer that big matches are won, more often than not, by the team who is stronger in both body and mind. In my opinion that's why so many players just fall short of being top class. I'd place Charlie and Tony in that category and every time I lined up against them I would try to exploit their weaknesses.

When we faced Chelsea it was a different ball game altogether as Kerry Dixon and David Speedie presented a different challenge. Kerry was a nutter who didn't know the meaning of fear and it was a relief to end up on the same side as him when I later signed for Chelsea. There were so many big, bustling centre forwards around at that time and Kerry was one of the toughest and most lethal finishers around. In my final season at Spurs he had some real ding-dong battles with Richard Gough. Kerry couldn't stand Goughie for some reason and was always challenging him to a fight. Even to this day he still says that he would love nothing better than to step into the boxing ring with my old Spurs and Rangers teammate. Maybe they could square up in a charity bout one day? That would be worth watching!

Kerry's striker partner also knew how to handle himself despite his diminutive stature, but it was also much easier to wind up David Speedie. He had the shortest fuse in football and I used to love getting under his skin because you knew he was certain to react. There was nothing subtle about pinching the back of his leg or poking him in the eye, but it still worked every time! David would lash out, pick up a booking and he then had to tread carefully or else his team would be playing out the match with ten men.

It used to be like that in training a lot of the time as well and I remember when I was at Chelsea we had a youngster coming through the ranks called Graeme Le Saux. Even as a lad he had all the attributes to be a top-class player but he was such a wimp. Graeme couldn't handle the physical aspect of the game and that's why the club released him. To his credit he worked on that part of his game and he eventually became a big success second time round at Stamford Bridge and forged a successful international career.

The pitfall of being a self-styled enforcer was that there were always plenty of forwards who wanted to prove they were even tougher than you. Also, if you were going to dish it out you had to be prepared to take it, so cuts, bruises and broken bones came with the territory. With Maxi knowing how to look after himself as well we deliberately set out to wind-up and intimidate the opposition.

One of our favourite ploys was to wait for the first high ball, ignore the ball completely, and then place the nut in the back of the centre forward's head. It hurt like hell, but it caused them even more pain. After that you knew he would have one eye on you every time he went for a header and his mind wouldn't be fully focused on the game. You tried to put them off their own game as much as you could and sometimes little advantages like that were the difference between winning and losing matches.

Two decades ago the first tackle was always free. The referee rarely, if ever, brought out his cards for your first challenge. Defenders knew that so you made the most of it. It was the ideal opportunity to signal your intent and give whoever you were marking a taste of what was to come. I don't mean going over the top of the ball or anything like that, but if the player didn't limp for a little bit when he got to his feet then you hadn't hit him hard enough.

Recently I was listening to Ray Wilkins, who made the point that the current Spurs team wouldn't win anything because they are a soft touch. He said they had some sublimely talented individuals although they lacked an animal like Graham Roberts. I think he meant it in a complimentary way. The successful Spurs team I played in was jam-packed with skill in the shape of Ossie Ardiles, Glenn Hoddle and Ricky Villa, but while we sometimes lacked a bit of bite in the middle of the park there was no way anybody would steamroller over our defence. The players who used to give us the most problems were nippy little strikers who were lighting fast over five yards. People like Tony Cottee were a nightmare to play against. I much preferred the tough guys.

Spurs had a nasty, ruthless streak at the back and every team needs that if they want to be successful at the highest level. All the best sides knew how to handle themselves and that was certainly the case with the great Liverpool team of the eighties that swept all before them. You wouldn't necessarily mark down Kenny Dalgish and Ian Rush as tough customers, but they could dish it out with the best of them. Kenny was particularly adept at leaving his foot in if you'd just cleared the ball. It didn't look much and the ref rarely saw it, but he was a clever bugger who knew exactly what he was doing.

Rush was exactly the same. That's probably why you rarely saw either of them complain when they got fouled. They accepted it was part and parcel of the game and just waited to seek revenge.

However, the master of that team was Graeme Souness. Here was a man who didn't take any prisoners. Of all the players I've played with and against Souness was the most complete. He had everything – technical ability, skill, ruthlessness, vision, toughness, determination and, most of all, arrogance. Souness knew he was the best and every time he stepped on the park he wanted to prove it. When I played with him at Rangers he strutted around like a preening peacock, but he could pull it off because he had so much class.

Vinnie Jones is a name that often crops up when you talk about hard men, but he wasn't in the same league as Souness. As far as I was concerned Vinnie was a talentless idiot. He was more hatchet man than hard man on the football pitch, yet the media made him out to be the scariest guy on the planet. I played against Wimbledon's Crazy Gang a couple of times when I was at Spurs and he just ran about the pitch like a nutcase. There's a difference between being hard and being reckless. Too often Vinnie was the latter and the number of times he went over the ball was disgraceful. He was as subtle as a sledgehammer and didn't have the ability to back up his thuggery. That's why he was red-carded so many times.

I remember being sent off as I was being carried off against Wimbledon, although it had nothing to do with Vinnie. It was near the end of the match and Lawrie Sanchez had hit me at knee height. I collapsed to the ground, but as I was going down I swung at him with a right hook. The ref dismissed Lawrie and as I was being carried from the pitch on a stretcher he showed me a red card as well. Lawrie then came into our dressing room and said: 'No hard feelings mate.' That was the end of the matter and we moved on.

Ex-Wimbledon striker John Fashanu was another formidable opponent although he must have taken a real dislike to Spurs. After knocking Gary Stevens out cold in a challenge he dislocated Gary Mabbutt's eye from its socket with a flying elbow. Fash was one of the most uncompromising strikers I faced although the hardest of all was probably Mick Harford.

Mick ended his career at Wimbledon although it was when he was at Luton we enjoyed some good tussles. He was an old-fashioned centre forward, who would run through a brick wall if he thought it would get him a goal. I remember the first time I encountered him at Kenilworth Road. I knew all about Mick's reputation as a tough nut and I was curious to find out whether there was any substance to it.

I started off with a knee in the back and then gave him a good crack to the back of the head when we were defending a Luton corner. Every time Mick got the ball I was all over him like a rash and after cementing him half a dozen times he just looked at me with complete disdain and said: 'Is that your best shot mate?'

I continued to kick him for the remainder of the first half and he didn't bat an eyelid. However, after the break he got me back with interest. I was defending a long free-kick into the box when he elbowed me in the kidneys. I tried to make out that it didn't hurt, although I'm sure my face turning purple was a bit of a giveaway. I was doubled over in agony and Mick just cut me a withering look. He didn't say a word. He was tall and gangly, but strong as an ox with it. They don't make them like him any more, which is a crying shame.

Manchester United's Norman Whiteside was cut from the same cloth although he was a far more talented player than

Mick. Big Norman had played in two World Cup Finals by the time he was 22 which is an incredible achievement. Coming into the game young he quickly learned how to look after himself. He was a frightening sight when he was coming at you full tilt and on his day he was almost impossible to handle.

A fearsome competitor, Norman had the heart of a lion and was one of those players who was simply unwilling to accept defeat. Virtually every time I came off the pitch after Spurs played Man United I was covered in bruises and they didn't come from his team-mates Jesper Olsen and Gordon Strachan! It was a tragedy his career was cut short through injury. I think Norman was simply too brave for his own good.

His Old Trafford colleague Mark Hughes was another tough customer and of all the players I've faced in twenty-odd years of football, Sparky was the most difficult opponent. Off the park he's one of the nicest guys you could ever wish to meet. On it he was hell to play against. Mark had formidable strength, outstanding technical ability, two great feet, he was phenomenal in the air and he could also mix it with the best of them. He was every defender's worst nightmare.

As for tough teams I always found Ipswich a proper handful. With guys like Terry Butcher, Russell Osman, Paul Mariner and Eric Gates in their line-up, Bobby Robson's men were always up for a good scrap. Every time we played them at the start of the eighties it was like World War III. There was always so much ill-feeling and animosity between the two sets of players and it made for explosive encounters.

Grudges were always carried over from previous matches and it was usually Gates who I found myself tangling with. He was always cocksure of himself at Portman Road in front of his own fans, but every time he came to White Hart Lane myself and Paul Miller would take it in turns to boot lumps out of him. It was survival of the fittest and I'm surprised there was anybody left standing at the end of 90 minutes.

During my spell in Scotland there were no proper hard cases. Celtic had plenty of good footballers, but I found Aberdeen were a much tougher proposition. As a defensive unit Brian Irvine, Alex McLeish, Willie Miller and Stuart McKimmie were formidable. If it came down to a physical contest they could handle most centre forwards without too many problems. They did finally meet their match when Rangers signed Mark Hateley. Big Mark was an awesome competitor and he was capable of scaring the living daylights out of the most hardened defenders.

I first encountered Mark when he was a teenager at Portsmouth. Understandably he was a bit naive then, but he learned how to look after himself following spells at AC Milan and Monaco. By the time he joined Rangers he was the complete package and if he became involved in a scrap with any of his peers then I'm pretty certain he would never come off second best.

Throughout my career I was extremely fortunate to line-up alongside some terrific talents and on the after-dinner circuit the question I most frequently get asked is: 'Who is the best player you've ever played with?' In a one-off game it has to be Diego Maradona. Not many people remember, but the South American genius actually turned out for Spurs back in 1984.

Ossie Ardiles had been granted a benefit match which was staggering considering he had only been at the club for a few years and was the highest paid player at White Hart Lane. Anyway, we played Inter Milan and Ossie had arranged for Maradona, who was with Napoli at the time, to come over and play. I remember him sitting in the dressing room before the match and Ossie asked him to show us all a few tricks. His ball juggling skills had us all gasping in amazement and he even continued playing keepy-up while signing autographs and posing for pictures with all the Spurs office staff.

In the game he was mesmerising and while it was only a friendly kick-about it was obvious you were in the presence of someone truly special. He was only a young lad at the time and he wasn't yet a global superstar, yet he still had this aura surrounding him. It was a privilege to be on the same pitch as him that night.

Maradona apart, there was nobody who could touch Glenn Hoddle. As far as I'm concerned, no British footballer in the modern era could hold a candle to Glenn. He was in a class of his own. His ability was scary and I don't think there will ever be another player who combines poise, balance, vision and an extraordinary shooting ability to such great effect on a football pitch. Glenn made the sublime look simple. He could crash shots into the top corner from 40 yards without any back lift.

A lot of Spurs and England fans reckon Gazza was a better player for club and country although I would have to disagree. There's no doubt Gazza was an exceptional talent, but Glenn truly was a genius. It still flabbergasts me that he only won 53 caps for his country and I just couldn't understand why he never really got the full backing of the different international managers he played under.

I remember being in the same England team as Glenn for a game against France at the Parc des Princes in Paris. Michel Platini scored twice in a 2-0 victory although after the match he couldn't stop raving about the exceptional talents of his midfield counterpart. Platini believed Glenn would have won 150 caps for his country if he'd been French. It was a travesty England didn't shape their team around Glenn as he was the one player of his generation who could open up any defence. Platini was the focal point of the French team and Maradona filled the same role for Argentina. Both won major championships in the late 1970s and 80s and I genuinely believe England would have followed suit if only they'd placed their trust in Glenn Hoddle.

Instead they shipped him out to the right- or left-hand side and asked him to run up and down the flank. That wasn't Glenn's game and it was to the detriment of the country. I don't recall there being any personality clash at the time as Glenn was a top bloke when he played for Spurs. He was always regarded as one of the boys. Now I think he sees himself as an outsider.

When we were at White Hart Lane together we used to go out for a few pints in Epping Forest every Thursday night without fail. However, he changed completely when he joined Monaco. He immersed himself in Christianity, stopped drinking and became a totally different person. His beliefs would eventually cost him his job as England manager when he suggested in a newspaper article that disabled people were being punished for sins in a previous life.

Glenn's religion became an easy stick for his detractors to beat him with, which is a shame because the squad he took to the 1998 World Cup should have been capable of going all the way. Instead, they returned with tails between their legs and Glenn standing accused of allowing his personal beliefs to spill over into his professional life.

Steve McManaman compared Glenn's training camps to a cult and accused him of favouring players who chose to embrace a faith healer called Eileen Drewery who he introduced to the England camp. Now I don't profess to know much about Christian evangelism and everyone is entitled to their beliefs, but I just don't recognise Glenn any more. Whenever all the old Spurs lads meet up at the various reunion nights the club organise, he always appears distant. He's become a loner and an outsider. That's a pity as it would be great to see the old Glenn back.

8

GLASGOW GREEN!

Five days before Christmas 1986 I had an early night as we were playing Chelsea the following afternoon and I was in the team. Deep down I knew it was only a matter of time before I left Spurs, but games against your biggest rivals are something special and I was determined not to let anybody down before I left White Hart Lane.

It was a good job I decided to get some extra kip because I was to get an unexpected early-morning alarm call from the man I despised more than any other in football. It was 6am when my phone started ringing and nine times out of ten it's never good news when you get a call at that time of the day. There were a million different thoughts rushing through my head as I rushed downstairs to answer it. Instinctively you think something is wrong and I was just praying that nothing had happened to my mum or dad because both of them had recently been ill.

When I eventually picked up the receiver my initial feeling was one of relief quickly followed by surprise, and then disgust. I was just glad my parents were OK although I just couldn't comprehend why David Pleat was calling me at such a ridiculous hour. There was no 'hello' and we didn't exchange any pleasantries.

His first words were: 'You've been sold, so don't turn up tomorrow and don't come back to the club.' He started to tell me that somebody else from Spurs would be in touch to sort out the arrangements although I was so angry I just slammed the phone down and started cursing and swearing as I stormed back upstairs. Part of me was delighted to be finally shot of Pleat, but I couldn't believe he had the audacity to pull a pathetic stunt like that. If it was a life or death emergency then you could understand it but you don't get phone calls at that time in the morning from a football club saying you have been sold.

I was later informed by someone at Ibrox that he'd agreed a deal with Souness at 8pm the previous night. I don't know that for certain, but I wouldn't put it past him. Rangers had first made a bid for me almost a month before and virtually every day I would visit Pleat in his office in an attempt to get the matter resolved. I wanted to leave, he wanted me to leave, yet he seemed determined to make life as awkward as possible for me.

There was even one point during the unfortunate saga when I told him there was no way I could play for a manager I didn't respect. I'd reached the end of my tether before a match with Watford and just stormed out. Professional pride got the better of me when I calmed down and I did return to play, but that was one of my last matches for Spurs.

Following my early-morning alarm from Pleat I got another call from Spurs at noon saying the club secretary, Peter Day, would pick me up and take me to the airport as we were both booked on a flight from Heathrow to Glasgow. In Scotland, Rangers secretary Campbell Ogilvie was there to meet us and after taking us to our hotel we arranged to meet with Graeme at Ibrox the following morning.

It should have been a formality as the clubs had agreed a fee and, following our preliminary discussions, I was happy with the terms on offer. However, on our way to the stadium Peter said that we had a bit of a problem. When I penned my last deal at Spurs I'd received a £30,000 signing-on fee, but they were now trying to claim it was a loan and they wanted it back. I told him there was no chance of that happening so we might as well turn round and catch the first flight back to London as I wouldn't be going anywhere.

I had a pretty good idea who was behind it and while I would have been gutted to miss out on joining Rangers, there's no way I was going to be messed about. If that's the way certain individuals at Spurs wanted to conduct business then I would have returned and played out the next three years of my contract in the reserves if I had to. Thankfully, it never reached that stage and while there was an impasse for a little while, Rangers finally agreed to pay an extra £30,000 on the transfer fee.

On the Monday I passed a medical before heading back south to collect my belongings and say goodbye to my team-mates at Spurs. But, just for good measure, there was another little surprise when I turned up at White Hart Lane. Outside the main entrance there were two black bin liners filled with all my boots and training gear. I wasn't even allowed in to say my farewells to the tea ladies never mind the guys I'd shared a dressing room with for the last seven years. I'd given

94

everything for Spurs, played 287 games for them and helped them win the UEFA Cup and two FA Cups, and this was the thanks I got. Even at the time I didn't feel any animosity towards the club because I knew who was responsible.

We'd never seen eye-to-eye and from the moment he took over from Peter Shreeve, Pleat made it crystal clear I wasn't going to be part of his long-term plans. That's fair enough as every manager has his own ideas about certain players, but there was no need to be so obnoxious about it. I doubt that Irving Scholar would say that appointing David Pleat was the best decision he ever made. I'd certainly say it was one of the worst.

Even when I signed for Rangers he just couldn't let it go. I remember reading the newspapers a few days later when Pleat did an article saying that I never did anything for Spurs apart from kick people and I would do exactly the same in Scotland. That probably hurt more than all the other pathetic stunts he pulled as it was a slur on my ability as a footballer. It was below the belt although I shouldn't really have expected anything else.

Football's a small world, but it wasn't until a few years ago when I was manager at Boreham Wood that our paths crossed again. I was filling up my car at a petrol station when he pulled up alongside me. 'Hello, Graham. How are you?' he said with a big smile on his face, although you could tell by the tone of his voice that there was nothing sincere about his greeting. I turned round and told him to be careful parking next to the kerb as you never know what you might pick up. It was a reference to his penchant for driving around the seedy red-light districts of London.

They say what goes around comes around and I couldn't hide my delight when he was forced to resign from Spurs, after only a year in charge, because of his extra-curricular activities. Pleat was cautioned by police for kerb crawling. Dirty old man.

I have so little respect for him and wouldn't piss on him if he was on fire. Thankfully I haven't bumped into him since although every time I hear his irritating little voice when he's commentating on the Champions League I want to put my foot through the television. He's a total prat and the biggest arsehole I ever had the misfortune to meet. Still, while I was gutted to leave Spurs I was excited at the prospect of playing for Rangers.

On the morning I signed, there were a few hundred supporters outside Ibrox and I immediately struck up a rapport with them. Rangers were big news south of the border. Since Souness had been appointed player/manager everybody was talking about them and there was a great deal of excitement about Scottish football.

Before Souness arrived on the scene, hardly anybody south of Hadrian's Wall bothered about the Old Firm. But, suddenly there was a huge buzz surrounding Rangers and Celtic and I wanted to be part of the revolution. In the Spurs dressing room we always used to talk about what was going on at Ibrox and Chris Waddle made no secret of the fact he wanted to play for Rangers. Glenn Hoddle was a big Celtic fan, but we never held that against him. Chris was a Gers fanatic and I think not getting the chance to play for them was one of the biggest regrets of his career.

I'd always had an affinity for Rangers as well although not

to the same extent as Chris who was a proper Bluenose. They were always my Scottish team when I was growing up although I didn't get to see them in the flesh until the 1986 League Cup Final against Celtic.

From the moment Richard Gough signed for Spurs all he ever went on about was the passion of an Old Firm match. Most of the guys in our dressing room had played in plenty of massive matches and been involved in loads of local derbies with Arsenal so I think they just took what he was saying with a pinch of salt. However, the more Goughie talked about Rangers v Celtic games, the more intrigued I became. I was determined to find out for myself what all the fuss was about so I was over the moon when Goughie got myself and Chris tickets for the game at Hampden.

The three of us flew up to Glasgow on Sunday morning and headed straight to the Sportsman's Pub in Paisley Road West for a spot of breakfast – three pints of lager and a roll and square sausage. We'd only crossed the border but I was already thinking we were on another planet. It was only 11am, but the place was absolutely heaving. The atmosphere was incredible. I'd never witnessed anything like this before and we were in the boozer with kick-off still over three hours away.

Quite a few punters recognised us on the way to Hampden and were kind enough to give us some Rangers scarves in exchange for our autographs. When the action got underway I realised what Goughie meant when he told us this was the biggest and best derby in the world. I'd played in plenty of North London derbies, and I'd been involved in Scotland v England internationals. Neither of those contests were for the faint hearted but they didn't come close to this. The only comparison was the UEFA Cup Final against Anderlecht, and this was only a Skol Cup Final.

Our seats were in the Main Stand, just behind the directors' box. It was the best view in the house and I was enthralled by every kick of that final. Rangers won 2-1 thanks to a great goal from Ian Durrant and an ice-cool penalty kick from Davie Cooper. I was absolutely shattered just watching the game and I couldn't begin to imagine what playing in a match of this magnitude would be like. Unbelievably, although completely unknown to me at the time, I would be lining up for Rangers in the next Old Firm match two months later.

After the game we headed back to the Sportsman's for a few more pints before grabbing the last shuttle back to London. That trip definitely made me think about the possibility of a move north at some stage in my career although not for one minute did I imagine it would all happen so quickly.

Fate, however, was about to intervene. On the flight home I was sitting beside Graeme Souness's brother-in-law and I was telling him how much I fancied giving it a go in Glasgow. He said he would pass my number on and, incredibly, I got a call from Souness about a week later. I told him I was serious about playing for Rangers and the wheels for the move north were put in motion. Maybe there's some truth in the saying that what's for you won't pass you by.

My debut against Dundee United on Boxing Day was also a special occasion for my first wife Ann and my little girl Hollie, who was only three at the time. This was a huge move for the whole family and Ann was desperate for all of us to be accepted. I'll be forever grateful to her for all the support she gave me when we uprooted from London and became part of the English revolution that was going on in Glasgow.

Understandably she wanted to make the right impression at her first game because, having been to plenty matches when I was at Tottenham, she knew the competition amongst the WAGS in the fashion stakes was usually as fierce as the competition for places on the pitch. Ann knew all eyes would be on her and Hollie so she was anxious to make sure the pair of them looked their best. She wanted to make a real effort as we'd just moved to Scotland so she bought Hollie a little tartan dress. It was Black Watch tartan which is predominantly blue with a little bit of green. And to complete the outfit Ann got her a little pair of green shoes. This game was a big deal for both of us and when I kissed her goodbye that morning I remember her being as proud as punch. She was also completely oblivious to the furore Hollie's footwear was about to cause.

There was a special lounge at Ibrox set aside for the wives and families of the players, the management, staff and the directors. Ann didn't know anybody yet so she was apprehensive beforehand, as most people would be in that situation. It's always awkward and while I must have been to thousands of functions over the years I still hate that initial ten minutes when you walk into a room and don't know anybody.

Once the ice is broken and the first person starts chatting to you then everything is normally fine. On this occasion one of the first people to come across and introduce themselves to Ann was the chairman's wife, who reprimanded her about the colour of Hollie's shoes. Very politely she was informed that green wasn't the appropriate dress code. Ann was cut to the bone and couldn't believe someone had actually taken offence at what a three-year-old was wearing.

She broke down in tears when I met her after the game and, at first, I thought it was because she was so pleased I'd played well on my debut and we'd won. The crowd had been chanting my name and I was on a real high after making such an impressive start. I kept telling her not to worry about it, but I could clearly see was quite distressed by the whole episode. I'd only played one game and already Ann was beginning to wonder what she'd let herself in for.

I was determined not to let one flippant remark spoil our day as I immediately sensed this could be the start of something special. When we got back to the hotel we had a bottle of champagne to celebrate and tried to forget about it.

On the park my debut couldn't have gone any better. I partnered Terry Butcher in central defence and the fact that we'd played with each other for England helped enormously. I didn't normally get nervous before games although, for some reason, I was shaking like a leaf when we walked out of the tunnel into a deafening wall of noise. Fortunately I made a couple of hard tackles early doors and that helped settled me down and get the crowd on my side. They were chanting my name and when something like that happens it gives you an enormous surge of confidence.

At half-time the score was 0-0 but we scored quickly after the break to take the tension out of the game. I played a major part in the opener by breaking up an attack after dispossessing Paul Sturrock and bursting forward. I tried to exchange a one-two with Ally McCoist and while Dave Narey got there before him, his pass back was woefully short and I got there just in front of their goalkeeper Billy Thompson. I squared it to Coisty who slotted it into the empty net. Ten minutes later Robert Fleck made it 2-0 and I was off to a winning start.

More importantly, I'd made a big impression on the crowd as they could see what sort of player I was. It can be difficult winning over the Rangers fans and even legends like Coisty and Mark Hateley took a while before they were finally welcomed into the fold. I was off and running and now there was the small matter of my first Old Firm game.

Celtic were the visitors to Ibrox on New Year's Day and with both of us in the race for the title this was a real six pointer. I was glad I'd been to Hampden a few months earlier as it at least gave me an inkling of what to expect. On the morning of the match I remember going to a little bookies' shop just off Byres Road with Davie Cooper although the rest of the day was pretty much a blur. The pace of the game was phenomenal and I'd barely had time to draw breath when the referee was blowing the final whistle.

The other thing that stands out was Souness producing a midfield masterclass. He ran the show as we strolled to a 2-0 victory. Conditions were horrendous with sleet and snow making it difficult to play football but it didn't hinder Souness. We were 2-0 up at half-time with Fleck giving us the lead and Coisty doubling our advantage when Pat Bonner fumbled a Souness cross and dropped it right at his feet. We coasted through the second period with Celtic unable to get near us. Time for another bottle of champagne although it's just as well I savoured it because that was the only time I was on the winning side in an Old Firm match.

That night we went out for a meal with a couple of friends who'd come up from London. Just after the waiter took our order, the Maitre d' came over and said: 'Mr Roberts, do you mind leaving?'

I said: 'I've only just arrived and haven't even had my meal yet.'

He replied: 'Well we've been asked if you would leave because they won't sit in the same restaurant as you.'

I asked who he was talking about, and when I looked up, there were about twenty people on this big long table. They were obviously Celtic fans who were a bit pissed off after we'd just given them a proper beating, but while I should just have got up and walked out I said: 'Tough. Our money is as good as theirs and we are going nowhere.'

My friends thought they'd been taken back in time to the deep south of America when segregation was in place. I wasn't too bothered and had no problem enjoying my meal, but I could tell Ann and our friends felt a bit uncomfortable throughout the evening. When we left the restaurant and jumped into our friends' car some of the group followed us out and tried to tip the vehicle over. Ann was hysterical by this stage and I was starting to panic a bit as well because you just never know what some people are capable of. I told my mate just to put his foot down and when he knocked one of them over and sent him spinning into the gutter where he belonged, the rest of them got the message and did a runner. Welcome to Glasgow.

On the park I'd made the perfect start to my Ibrox career and those two victories set the tone for the remainder of the campaign as Rangers closed in on their first title for nine years. When I joined we were eight points behind Celtic with two games in hand, but a couple of wins for us combined with a pair of defeats for them helped us reduce the gap considerably.

We'd started to gather momentum just at the right time and while Coisty and Flecky were scoring goals for fun at one end of the pitch we were becoming impossible to score against at the other. From November to January, Chris Woods set a British shut-out record when he went 1196 minutes in all competitions without conceding a goal. His amazing record is still standing 15 years later. I don't think it will ever be broken.

9

PARADISE AT PITTODRIE

The Grosvenor Hotel in the West End was my home for three months when I first moved to Glasgow. It wasn't ideal but the staff treated me and my family like royalty throughout our stay and that helped enormously. Rangers also used the hotel as base because Graeme Souness always liked the players to spend the night away from their families before matches. Even although I stayed at the hotel full-time I still had to leave Ann and Hollie on a Friday night and join the rest of the lads. The gaffer didn't want to make any allowances regardless of my domestic situation and I was quite happy with the arrangement as it guaranteed me a full night's sleep away from the little one.

Davie Cooper was my room-mate and sharing with him was an unforgettable experience. Coop was one of the greats of the game and it was a travesty he was taken away from us at such an early age. Alongside Glenn Hoddle he was the most talented footballer I've ever played with and that was quite an achievement considering he didn't have a right foot. But he certainly made up for it with a left peg that could open a can of beans. In training Coop could do tricks which would leave the rest of the lads gasping in amazement. He also had a heart of gold and if you were in the trenches you'd want Coop alongside because he would never let you down. However, he was also the biggest moaner God put on this earth. No wonder the players nicknamed him 'Albert' after Albert Tatlock, a miserable old git who used to be in *Coronation Street*.

We got on like a house on fire and you just had to take his moaning with a pinch of salt. Coop was only ever content when he was complaining about something. Every time I made him a cup of tea he moaned. There was either too much sugar or not enough milk. It could have been the perfect brew ever made but he still would never tell you that. When we went for breakfast there was always something not cooked to his liking and usually the toast wasn't brown enough.

Coop was a massive punter and our Saturday morning routine was always the same. Breakfast, read the papers and then pop down to William Hill's to back a few horses and put a coupon on. He always had a tip from someone although, to give him his due, he did win me quite a few bob during our spell as room-mates. It was a great arrangement which, unfortunately, didn't last too long as he landed me right in it and almost led to my missus divorcing me. She eventually did a few years later, but on this occasion I was an innocent party.

Coop always had an eye for a pretty girl and at the time he was having a dalliance with a former Miss Scotland. She used to come to the hotel on a Friday night so, as I didn't much fancy playing gooseberry, I would bunk down with Ian Durrant or one of the other lads. This went on for a few weeks until Coop's cover was blown when the story appeared in the newspapers. 'Rangers star in secret trysts with top model at the Grosvenor,' screamed the front page headlines. I'll never forget the look on Ann's face as she threw a copy of the newspaper down on the table and asked me to explain myself. She thought that because I was sharing with Coop I'd been involved in some sort of threesome! It took a lot of explaining on my part, but I think she eventually believed me. Colin West became my room-mate for the rest of the season.

Looking back I will be eternally grateful to Coop, not for tossing me out of my room every Friday night, but for explaining exactly what it meant to be a Rangers player. Nobody was more passionate about the club than Davie Cooper and it was Coop who made me fully appreciate what pulling on the famous Light Blue jersey was all about. The previous nine seasons when Rangers failed to win the championship had left him scarred as he'd been at the club longer than anybody else when I arrived. That's why I wanted to win the league title that year, as much for him as for myself.

My incredible start to life up north continued in our next game at Motherwell when I scored the only goal of the game to keep us on the coat tails of leaders Celtic. It was a sensational 40-yard effort which flashed past the keeper like an Exocet missile and was one of the sweetest strikes of my life.

The wins just kept on coming and we leapfrogged Celtic at the top of the league when we beat Hamilton 2-0 at Ibrox. But I suffered my first setback when I was red-carded in controversial circumstances. I had already been booked when I tackled Albert Craig on the touchline and he started rolling about as if he'd been shot. I'd hardly touched him and there was no way it was a foul never mind a caution. However, the referee was conned by his theatrics and muggins was shown a second yellow card. As I was walking off he lifted up his strip to reveal a Celtic strip underneath and kissed the badge right in front of the Copland Road. I thought: 'You sad bastard.' He was sniggering away to himself as I trooped down the tunnel.

Ian Durrant had seen what went on and was giving him some serious verbals. I'd only been in the bath a couple of minutes when Durranty arrived to join me. I wasn't surprised to learn he'd been red carded for doing Craig.

We were both suspended the following week and returned for the Scottish Cup clash at Ibrox, ironically against Hamilton. Now, even to this day, I still don't know how we didn't win that match. But the bottom line is that we didn't and we will forever be remembered for being on the end of what was arguably one of the greatest giant-killing acts in Scottish football history.

We should have been out of sight before half-time as we must have created a dozen clear cut chances to break the deadlock. However, Hamilton's veteran goalkeeper Dave McKellar was having the kind of afternoon you can only dream about. It was real Roy of the Rovers stuff as he pulled off a string of top-class saves to keep his team in the game. We beat Hamilton four times in the Premier League that season and there was never any suggestion that we treated them lightly or failed to give them enough respect.

The score should have been 10-1 as we battered them for almost 90 minutes, but they had one attack all afternoon and scored. Dave McPherson had one lapse of concentration when he allowed the ball to run under his foot and from being a nobody, Adrian Sprott became a superstar overnight when he swept the ball past Chris Woods. Our hopes of completing the Treble went up in smoke and we had to face the consequences.

Souness was never one for a quiet period of reflection and he blew a gasket after the game. You couldn't blame him really as he was the one who would carry the can for one of the most humiliating defeats in the club's history. When he came in after the match he put his boot through a television set that had the misfortune to be in his line of fire.

It was a small television which sat on a table just as you came into the dressing room and after every game Doddie the kitman would switch it on so we could watch the other results coming in. 'Who fucking put that on?' Souness barked as he stormed in with steam coming out of his ears. One minute James Alexander Gordon was going through the final scores, the next the TV had exploded and was lying smashed to smithereens on the floor. That just summed up Souness though. He was a bad loser, but that's why he was such a great player. He was a winner through and through. Walter eventually calmed him down and told us to make sure we made up for this by winning the title.

Hamilton's victory was front and back page news the following day and as a player you get the feeling the whole country is laughing at you after an upset like that. I'm sure half of the nation were pissing their pants although there was a championship still to be won so we couldn't mope about feeling sorry for ourselves.

The gaffer gave us all a few days off and when we returned to training the following week the Hamilton match was never mentioned. It was consigned to the history books, yet somehow I don't think any of us who were involved that afternoon will ever be allowed to forget it.

In many ways I think our Scottish Cup exit played a huge part in us pipping Celtic to the title as we didn't have any other distractions. The League was our main goal and that was the sole focus for the last four and a half months of the season. We proved what we were made of in our next game against Hearts. Tynecastle has always been one of the most difficult venues to get a result and it would be a real test of our resilience. That day we really stepped up to the plate and produced our best performance of the season. We tore Hearts to shreds and ran out comprehensive 5-2 winners. The Hamilton debacle hadn't left a lasting impression and it was after our stunning victory in Edinburgh that I became convinced we would claim the championship.

I had to climb out of my sick-bed for that game after being floored by a nasty bout of food poisoning. On the Wednesday before the game I was attending a charity dinner at the Grosvenor with Ann. About 5pm I was starving so I ordered an omelette from room service to keep me going. What a bad move that turned out to be. I'd only just arrived at the function and they were serving the starter when I started to feel awful. I rushed upstairs to our room and when Ann came in about 15 minutes later she found me being violently sick everywhere. She called for a doctor, who took one look at me and ordered an ambulance. I spent the night in the Southern General Hospital where they discovered I'd become ill after eating rotten ham in my omelette. There was no way I could train on the Thursday or the Friday before the game but the gaffer was still anxious for me to play on the Saturday against Hearts at Tynecastle. We won easily, with Coop having a blinder and I just knew that we would beat Celtic to the title.

By the time we faced them again at Parkhead in April we were four points clear and we knew a win would give us an unassailable lead. The pressure was on them, but they responded magnificently to put the destiny of the title back in the melting pot. Celtic scored twice from the penalty spot in a deserved 3-1 success and with only a few games remaining there was only one point separating the Old Firm.

That result set up a nerve-shredding finale to the campaign and everybody was convinced it would inevitably go down to a last-day decider. On the penultimate week of the season we travelled to Pittodrie while Celtic were at home to Falkirk. A draw coupled with a defeat for our bitter rivals would hand us the title, but nobody realistically believed that would happen. We made the long trek north more in hope than expectation although our supporters certainly weren't thinking like that. They descended on Aberdeen in their droves with some of them paying up to £50 for a £5 ticket.

Pittodrie was a sea of red, blue and white that afternoon and you really struggled to pick out the Aberdeen fans in the capacity crowd. The punters must have had some sort of premonition because while I was confident we would win the league I was certain it would be the following weekend when we hosted St Mirren at Ibrox. But we knew a draw in the game with Aberdeen was the crucial one as they hated us and regardless of whether there was anything at stake for them, going to Pittodrie was always a real war of attrition. However, as we were certain of beating St Mirren on the last day of the season, the destiny of the league flag would ultimately be decided in Aberdeen.

The gaffer knew a draw would be enough and I'll never forget his team talk before we went out onto the pitch. He said: 'Let's keep it solid and don't give anything away. They will try to wind you up, so make sure you don't react as we can't afford anybody to get sent off.'

Twenty minutes into the game and Souness was red-carded for a shocking tackle. That set-back only helped fire us up even more and Terry Butcher sent the crowd wild when he put us ahead with a stunning bullet header from a Coop corner. But Aberdeen were intent on being the party poopers and Brian Irvine equalised in first-half injury time.

At half-time Souness never mentioned his sending-off. If it had been anybody else he would have gone through them like a dose of salts. He never apologised for leaving us to play out most of the match with ten men although we never expected him to. Souness was never ever wrong no matter what he did. That's just the way it was with him.

The second half was a dour affair with no further scoring and we were resigned to putting the champagne on ice until the following Saturday. But what followed was one of the most bizarre and surreal experiences of my life. There were a couple of minutes remaining when I heard a few muffled cheers.

I looked up and I could see some of our supporters jumping up and down. Loads of the fans had radios with them and they were listening to commentary on the Celtic game. Amazingly they had bottled it and Falkirk had beaten them 2-1. It was like a mass game of Chinese whispers as word from Parkhead filtered through to Pittodrie.

The players quickly cottoned on to what was happening and I remember dancing and high-fiving with Jimmy Nichol while our match was still going on. When the ref did blow his whistle all hell broke loose as the Rangers fans dashed on to the pitch. I've never seen so many grown men cry and as the scenes of unbridled joy unfolded you realised just how much it meant to the supporters. Over the past decade Rangers had been living in the shadow of Celtic, Aberdeen and Dundee United and now we had delivered them the holy grail. Rangers were back on top and it was a magnificent feeling to join in the over-exuberant celebrations with the supporters, who were our 11th man in the absence of the gaffer. When we needed some help during the second half when the tension was unbearable, they provided it.

It took me half an hour to reach the relative sanctuary of the dressing room although when I did make it down the tunnel I was minus my shirt, my shorts and my boots. I hope they found a good home. The coach journey home was pretty special and everybody was completely pissed by the time we reached Glasgow. Just after we left Aberdeen the gaffer summoned me down to the front of the bus and handed me a glass of champagne. 'Here's to the league title and your new contract, Robbo,' he said. When I signed, Souness said he would give me a wage rise if we won the championship and he proved as good as his word.

I was on a basic wage of £1000 a week although by the time we arrived back in Glasgow I was on £1500. Happy days. There was no chance of me spending any of it that night when we hit the town as we didn't have to put our hands in our pockets once. Everywhere we went there were queues of people buying us drinks. It was complete mayhem and I enjoyed every second of it.

Souness had delivered the goods in his first season in charge, just as he said he would, and we were presented with the trophy the following weekend after our game with St Mirren. The game, which we won 1-0, was a minor inconvenience because everybody just wanted to start celebrating again.

Ann got three T-shirts specially made for the occasion and after the game I posed proudly for the cameras with Terry Butcher and Chris Woods. They said: 'McRoberts, McButcher, McWoods PLC – Premier League Champions.'

At the end of it all I was emotionally and physically drained and just desperate to lie on a beach for a couple of months during the close season. However, before I could even think about a holiday I had a couple of commitments to fulfil. The first was an end of season tournament involving Liverpool and Maccabi Tel Aviv in Israel. After that I met up with Chris Waddle in the United States where we did some coaching clinics in Birmingham, Alabama and Tallahassee, Florida. We did that at the end of most seasons when we were at Spurs and afterwards our families would enjoy a holiday in Orlando. It was a good way of getting to visit different parts of America and we were always well rewarded.

That summer was particularly memorable and given that Chris was a huge Rangers punter I think, if anything, he celebrated their championship victory even more than me.

10

ROUGH JUSTICE

Since moving to Scotland things just couldn't have gone any better, on and off the field. Life was perfect. I'd helped Rangers win the championship for the first time in nine years while Ann and Hollie loved living in Helensburgh. Our lifestyle at that time was pretty idyllic. We could afford anything we wanted, and as a family, we were more settled than we'd ever been.

It was almost too perfect. Our happiness was shattered one Wednesday night when we all arrived home following a midweek game against Motherwell. We'd been broken into and the place had been completely trashed. They'd obviously long gone, but I still felt sick to the pit of my stomach that someone had violated our privacy and been through all our belongings. Anyone who has been unfortunate enough to go through the same experience will know exactly what I mean. Nothing was really missing and it looked as if the burglars had been spooked because all our valuables were still there. We didn't take any great comfort from that and Ann wanted us to move house straight away. She felt she could never feel safe again, but I managed to convince her that we would be letting the criminals win if we put the For Sale signs up. I wish I'd listened to her.

A couple of weeks later we were playing Aberdeen at Pittodrie, again it was a midweek match, but this time Ann stayed at home with Hollie. She was watching television and doing the ironing in the lounge while Hollie slept in her cot next door. There was a knock on the front door about 9.30pm and when she looked out it was the police.

'We've had a report of a burglary at this property,' they told her. My wife told them that couldn't possibly be the case as she'd been at home all night. The police asked if they could come in and have a look around just to make sure. As they walked into our bedroom it was a scene of complete devastation. All the clothes from the drawers and wardrobes were strewn across the floor and the window had been smashed. Ann realised most of her jewellery had been stolen while there was also about £1000 in cash missing.

There was always loads of money lying about the place because I fancied myself as a bit of an Arthur Daley at the time. I knew plenty of dodgy people from my time at Spurs and they could get their hands on anything you wanted whether it was televisions, washing machines or clothes. Sportswear was my biggest seller and biggest earner. Nike were the hottest trainer in town at the time and I used to get all the new versions before they were in the shops and flog them to the players.

The break-in was both a frightening and bizarre experience as the burglars must have had a bit of a conscience because they were the only ones who could possibly have called the police. My wife couldn't get hold of me because I was playing at the time so she phoned the club, who managed to get hold of the chairman. He arranged for a taxi to pick me up at

Pittodrie and take me back to Ibrox where I collected my car and drove home. I was so relieved nothing had happened to her and Hollie although, understandably, she was in a real state.

The story found its way into the newspapers – these things always do – and as I was walking to my car after our next home match against Hibs a few fans approached me. 'We read about your burglary and we're going to sort it out.' That's all they said and walked off. I didn't give it a second thought.

The following Sunday I was walking our collie dog, who hadn't even barked during the break-in, and pushing Hollie in her pram along the seafront at Helensburgh when a mini-bus load of Rangers supporters pulled up. I recognised the lads who'd spoken to me the previous week. They said: 'We told you we'd find out who robbed your house, Robbo. Just leave it with us and the matter will be resolved. We know who it was.' To be honest I didn't really take them too seriously and I thought they were just some well-meaning punters pretending to have a go at being private detectives. I thanked them out of courtesy and headed back to my house.

A few days later the police arrived back at my door and asked me if I knew anything about an alleged attack that had taken place in the town. While investigating a serious assault, the guy who'd been put in hospital confessed to the break-ins at my house. He'd suffered two broken legs and was in a pretty bad way. Now I've no idea how these fans found out and I don't really want to, but they'd taken it upon themselves to dish out their own form of justice.

It turned out that the bloke responsible was the taxi driver who used to regularly deliver our Chinese takeaways.

SHELL SUIT ROB! Me aged four, in my parents' garden wearing a dodgy looking tracksuit

HAIR RAISING: Winning another trophy with my youth team, Wildern Sky Blues. Can you spot me amongst this stylish lot?!

STRIKE ONE: Celebrating scoring my first goal for Spurs against Exeter in the FA Cup. Garth Crooks and Paul Miller join in

NO PAIN NO GAIN: Grimacing in agony with a bout of cramp in the 1981 FA Cup Final at Wembley. I'd had three teeth knocked out earlier in a clash with team-mate Chris Hughton

SWEET FA CUP: Posing alongside Glenn Hoddle with the FA Cup, my first major trophy, after beating Man City in a replay

BARCA BOY: Equalising against Barcelona in the 1982 European Cup Winners Cup Semi Final First Leg match at White Hart Lane

©PA Photos

TOP SPURS: Celebrating back-to-back FA Cup victories after beating QPR after a replay

RUUD AWAKENING: Tussling with a young Ruud Gullit as we thrashed Feyenoord en route to the 1984 UEFA Cup Final

©Mirrorpix.com

PARKS LIFE: Myself, Ossie Ardiles, Gary Stevens and Chris Hughton prepare to mob keeper Tony Parks after his decisive save in the 1984 UEFA Cup Final penalty shoot-out against Anderlecht

KINGS OF EUROPE: The proudest moment of my career. Captaining Spurs to UEFA Cup glory in front of our own fans at White Hart Lane

©PA Photos

HAPPY NEW YEAR: My Old Firm debut at Ibrox on January 1, 1987. Robert Fleck is mobbed after opening the scoring against Celtic

©PA Photos

©SNS Group

RED MIST: May 1987. Protesting as Graeme Souness is red carded at Pittodrie, on the day Rangers clinched the Premier League championship

©PA Photos

©The Daily Record

MacROBERTS: Ally McCoist gatecrashes the League championship celebrations with Rangers' 'English Connection' – myself, Chris Woods and Terry Butcher

BAWL BOY: Barking out instructions to my team-mates in the Rangers defence

LOSING THE PLOT: I'm dumbfounded as referee Jim Duncan sends off Chris Woods and Celtic's Frank McAvennie in one of the most controversial Old Firm clashes in history

CHOIRMASTER: Conducting the Rangers crowd in an Ibrox sing-song. My actions landed me in court, but I'd do the same again

COURT APPEARANCE: Arriving at Glasgow Sheriff Court with Chris Woods and Terry Butcher in April 1987, for the start of our 'show trial'

CLEVER TREVOR: Celebrating our dramatic cup victory with Trevor Francis

SCOT LUCK: Beating the Jocks 2-0 at Wembley in the 1983 Home Internationals final!

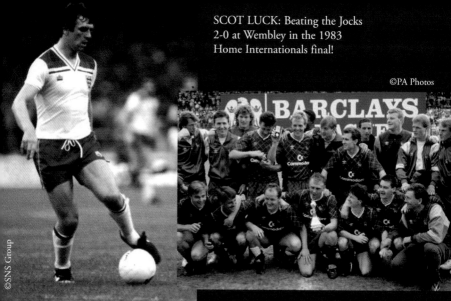

BLUE DO: May 1999. Chelsea celebrate after clinching the Division Two championship with a record 99 points and 99 goals

PAST MASTER: Spurs' old boys win the Carling Masters Five-A-Side Tournament at the London Arena. Celebrating with (l-r) Milija Aleksic, Chris Waddle, Glenn Hoddle, Paul Miller, Micky Hazard, Mark Falco, Gary Brook, Gary Stevens, Clive Allen and John Gorman

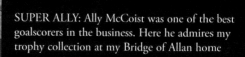

SUPER ALLY: Ally McCoist was one of the best goalscorers in the business. Here he admires my trophy collection at my Bridge of Allan home

CLYDE BOSS: With Clyde directors Len McGuire (left) and John Ruddy at the Marriott Hotel in Glasgow after being appointed the club's new manager

©SNS Group

©SNS Group

HUMBLING THE HOOPS: Eddie Malone challenges the legendary Roy Keane during our amazing Scottish Cup win over Celtic in January 2006

JUMPING FOR JOY: Going crazy on the touchline at the final whistle as the enormity of our giant-killing success sinks in

©PA Photos

©SNS Group

BULLY WEE: Celebrating with the players and the magnificent Clyde fans at the end of an incredible afternoon

DADDY'S GIRL: Larking about with my eldest daughter Hollie during my first spell in Scotland with Rangers

CLAN ROBERTS: Hollie, Sasha, and Ella pose with Luke following his passing out parade

GRANDAD: At my daughter's home with my grandson Joshua

Apparently he worked in tandem with his 13-year-old son and they targeted bungalows so the lad could squeeze through the small windows. It's not very politically correct, but I was delighted when the cops told me the burglar was in hospital and I'd like to thank the vigilante fans who sorted him out. It was nothing less than he deserved.

Incredibly, I spotted him about a month later while I was doing my shopping in Asda. I was pushing my trolley round the supermarket while he was getting pushed round in a wheelchair. I wanted to give him another beating, which wouldn't have been the smartest move, but Ann pulled me away and told me not to be so stupid. We never did get any of our jewellery or money back though.

We both loved living in Helensburgh and while it was a great environment to bring up kids there was no way we could continue living there after the break-ins. The club said they would take care of everything and within a few weeks they'd arranged for us to see a place in Bridge of Allan just outside Stirling. Terry Butcher and Chirs Woods both lived just around the corner so it sounded ideal.

It was an old sandstone, semi-detached villa which didn't look much from the outside and, as I recall, it didn't look much better inside to be honest. But the area was stunning and the potential was massive. An old woman had lived in the property all her life and I don't think it had seen a lick of paint for about 30 years. When she passed away her family put the house up for sale.

We were determined to buy the place and after our first viewing we went straight to the estate agent to make an offer. However, they us told it was closed bids and we needed to submit one before noon on the Friday. This was on the Wednesday morning. I didn't have a clue about the price of property in Scotland so I asked a few people at the club for some advice. On the Thursday I got a call from the chairman telling me to submit a bid of exactly £80,000 and the house would be mine. I asked him how he could be so certain when it was a closed auction. 'Call it an educated guess,' he said and put the phone down.

The following day I got a phone call from the estate agents telling me our bid had been successful. It was £5 more than the second highest offer! The chairman had pulled out all the stops once again, but he didn't stop there.

As the place was almost derelict there was no way we could move in straight away. Ann was anxious to leave Helensburgh as quickly as possible although I reckoned it would take at least six months to renovate our new house in Bridge of Allan. The chairman assured us he would have it looking like brand new within six weeks. And he didn't let us down. He arranged for a team of builders and decorators to work on it round the clock to make sure it was ready. The refurbishment cost £25,000, which was a massive amount of money twenty years ago, and the club paid every penny.

The transformation was like something out of the programme *Grand Designs*. It was amazing and every piece of furniture and every appliance was state of the art. It was, by a distance, the best house I've ever lived in, although unfortunately I didn't get to stay very long. Three months later I was slapped on the transfer list and was sold to Chelsea shortly afterwards. Getting £263,000 for a house I'd paid only £80,000 for less than a year earlier was some consolation. But selling the place was one of my biggest ever regrets. It was a stunning place and must be worth at least £1 million today. That would have been a nice little nest egg for my kids.

On the park, my second season at Rangers began well and there was no hint of the bitter disappointment that lay ahead when the club reached its third successive League Cup Final in October 1987. Rangers had a real stranglehold on the competition and there was no way we were going to give it up lightly – even when it looked like Aberdeen would be taking the trophy back up north. The final came just a week after the infamous Old Firm clash at Ibrox which landed me, Terry Butcher, Chris Woods and Frank McAvennie in court.

Terry and Woodsy were suspended following their red cards against Celtic so the gaffer handed me the captain's armband before we played Aberdeen. Nicky Walker took over in goal. It was an amazing honour to lead Rangers out at Hampden and I had no intention of being on the losing side. But, after being denied a winner's medal in the cruellest of circumstances in my only previous League Cup Final appearance – with Spurs when Liverpool scored a late winner after we'd been ahead – history looked set to repeat itself.

The game was an absolute classic with drama and tension from start to finish. We got off to the worst possible start when Nicky brought down Willie Falconer to concede an early penalty and Jim Bett stroked home the spot kick. Davie Cooper then equalised with one of the best free kicks I've ever seen, hammering a thunderous effort past Jim Leighton before the Aberdeen keeper even had time to move. Ian Durrant put us 2-1 ahead at the interval, but Aberdeen refused to lie down and John Hewitt made 2-2 after I made a hash of a clearance.

It looked like the Dons' name was on the trophy when Falconer put them back in front with ten minutes to go. However, as the clock ran out, I headed a Coop cross down to Robert Fleck and he slotted home to force extra-time and then penalties.

McCoist, Coop, Fleck and Trevor Francis all scored for us while Bett, Hewitt, and Peter Weir did the same for Aberdeen before Peter Nicholas, who I linked up with at Chelsea the following season, crashed his effort over the crossbar. Durranty made no mistake with the decisive kick and I went up the steps at Hampden to collect my second major honour just ten months after signing from Spurs.

We were on a roll and I thought a second league title was a formality. We were playing great football, confidence was sky-high, there was a terrific spirit in the camp and as well as scoring goals we rarely looked like conceding any. Then disaster struck when Terry Butcher broke his leg against Aberdeen. If I had a pound for the number of times I've heard people saying Terry's injury cost us the title that year, I'd be a millionaire.

Terry was our talisman at the time. He was an inspirational captain, a terrific leader and arguably the best central defender in Britain. But the bottom line is that we should have been able to cope without him. We had the strongest and most talented squad in the country and it was also jam packed with leaders.

Richard Gough, who had been playing right-back, was an ideal replacement at the heart of the defence and I'd like to think of myself as officer material. Coisty wasn't exactly slow at coming forward while Souness himself was also a real leader of men, more so on the pitch than off it. However, following another embarrassing Scottish Cup exit against Dunfermline, our season just nose-dived.

Looking back I think we were maybe all guilty of under-estimating Celtic that year and they deserve enormous credit for taking advantage of our situation and putting us under pressure. This time it was Rangers who cracked. When results started to go against us the manager seemed incapable of sorting out our problems. In fact, I think he exacerbated the situation by making a lot of bad judgement calls, particularly in the transfer market.

Souness was always regarded as a chequebook manager during his spell in charge at Ibrox although he also did his fair share of selling. At the turn of the year, the gaffer made two strange decisions which possibly had as much of a bearing on Celtic winning the Premier League as losing Big Terry. We were still well in the hunt for the title when he sold Mark Falco to Queen's Park Rangers for £350,000. Mark was a brilliant target man and his style of play was ideally suited to Scottish football. Fans didn't always notice the shift he put in, but he was a brilliant team player and all the lads loved playing alongside him because he was so unselfish. He scored some important goals during his short stint in Glasgow including a memorable strike against Dynamo Kiev in the European Cup. It didn't make any sense to let him go, but shortly after arriving from Watford he was on his way back to London.

Mark was a good mate as we'd been team-mates at Spurs for a while and I know he was gutted he never got the opportunity to prove himself with Rangers. Flogging him was bad enough, but to get rid of Robert Fleck a few weeks later beggared belief. There was a real clash of personalities between Fleck and the gaffer and the pair were always at loggerheads. When that happens with Souness there is only ever going to be one winner as myself and Terry would later find out to our cost.

Fleck had scored four hat-tricks the previous season and as a penalty box predator he was almost as good as Coisty. But that counted for nothing if you didn't see eye to eye with the gaffer so he was sold to Norwich for £600,000. In purely financial terms it was a good deal, however his departure left us woefully short in the striking department. To make matters worse, the deadline to register players for European competition had passed and we had the small matter of a European Cup quarter-final with Steaua Bucharest on the horizon.

Coisty was the only fit striker at the club although that was stretching the truth a bit far as he'd gone through a cartilage operation the previous week. The Romanians were there for the taking but, as far as I was concerned, Souness had allowed himself to put his ego ahead of the club's Euro aspirations. We lost 3-2 on aggregate and with that defeat went a golden opportunity to reach the semi-final of the European Cup.

11

CONDUCTOR OF THE CHOIR

Twenty years have come and gone since my infamous appearance at Glasgow Sheriff Court alongside my Rangers teammates Terry Butcher, Chris Woods and Celtic striker Frank McAvennie. In many ways it still feels like yesterday because it is one of the most talked about incidents in Old Firm history. The passage of time can heal many wounds but I still feel a huge sense of bitterness about the fall-out from an incredible Glasgow derby at Ibrox which led to me standing in the dock.

In many ways the Not Proven verdict against me was largely irrelevant because the Procurator Fiscal who brought the case against myself and the other guys achieved what he set out to do – and that was make a name for himself. At the time I thought the whole episode was farcical and two decades on I'm still of the same opinion.

The game itself was one of the most incident-packed and highly charged I've ever been involved in. It was mayhem from start to finish and I loved every minute. In my opinion the match – which ended in a 2-2 draw – was memorable for all the right reasons because this was what Old Firm derbies were all about. Two teams going at each other as if their lives depended on it. There was no quarter asked and no quarter given. Yes, there were three red cards, but there must have been hundreds of dismissals in the fixture since then and nobody has ended up in court over it.

Even now I can vividly recall virtually every kick of the ball during that game and the incident which kicked off the whole chain of events was relatively minor. Jimmy Phillips played a ball back to Chris Woods from the right-hand side and when he tried to pick it up McAvennie barged him into the back of the net. There was a big scuffle in the six-yard box and while it seemed like everybody apart from the Celtic keeper was involved there were no punches thrown. It was handbags at ten paces.

I can remember both Chris and Terry pushing McAvennie and telling him in no uncertain terms to 'fuck off' but McAvennie being McAvennie wanted to come back for more. Sensing Big Terry would probably have killed him I grabbed McAvennie by the throat and tried to haul him out of the way before it started to turn really nasty. He went down holding his face and when the whole brouhaha died down, the referee Jim Duncan came over and brandished a red card to McAvennie and Woodsy. I'm convinced if we'd had a stronger official in charge of the match nothing would have happened. He'd have sorted everything out and it would have blown over.

Instead we had a referee who exacerbated the problem because he simply was not up to dealing with a game of this magnitude. There are plenty of referees, Graham Poll springs immediately to mind, who just seem to want to make a name for themselves. But, in this instance, the whole occasion was just too big for Jim Duncan. Unsurprisingly I don't think he ever took charge of another Old Firm encounter.

When Woodsy went off I took over from him in goal as there were no substitute keepers back then. On a Friday in training I'd regularly play in goals because Woodsy fancied himself as a centre forward. I'd also played in goal for Spurs during an FA Cup tie when Ray Clemence got injured so it wasn't a completely alien experience. To be honest, I quite fancied myself as a goalie despite my lack of height although it quickly went wrong as I'd only been between the sticks a few minutes when Celtic went 1-0 ahead.

Andy Walker was played through and I remember running out to try and narrow the angle. But he hit it early and it went under my body and into the net. I felt like a complete pillock as I knew there's no way he would have scored if Woodsy was still on the pitch. Ten minutes later it would go from bad to worse as a breakdown in communication between myself and Terry helped Celtic take a 2-0 half-time lead. I came racing out of my goal to collect the ball, but Terry didn't hear my shout, which wasn't surprising given that the noise inside the stadium was deafening. He got his foot to the ball first and lobbed it straight over my head and into the net. At the other end of the park it would have been a deft touch, but this was a disaster.

Peter Grant then ran behind the goal and blessed himself. Now I've got nothing against any particular faith, but I don't think the middle of a passionate, powder-keg Old Firm derby is the appropriate time for that type of gesture. Given the circumstances that day, Peter's celebration was ill-advised to say the least because he knew more about these fixtures than anybody and he knew exactly what he was doing. But the Celtic punters loved it and they weren't slow to shower me with abuse either. Again I knew this cock-up wouldn't have happened if we had a proper keeper on the pitch and I was expecting a rollicking when I went in at the interval.

However, Souness and Walter were surprisingly calm in the dressing room. They were probably the only two people in the stadium who didn't seem caught up in the madness of what had just unfolded. They just told us to go back out and prove what we were made of. That was it. There were no histrionics or tea cups getting tossed about.

The reassuring team-talk appeared to work as we went out after the break and played some excellent football. Ally McCoist was again the man for the big occasion and quickly pulled a goal back, but while we were completely rampant we just couldn't get back on level terms. Midway through the half we won a corner and when Celtic keeper Alan McKnight caught the ball Terry fell over the top of him. McKnight started rolling around in agony and I knew exactly what was coming next. Terry had been booked for his part in the first half shenanigans and the referee just couldn't wait to produce a second yellow and then point him in the direction of the tunnel.

The second dismissal changed the course of the match and from being in total control we were suddenly on the back foot. They kept hitting us on the break as we charged forward and I was just praying the ball wouldn't come near me. But, with a few minutes left, I started to come for an Owen Archdeacon cross and then realised I wasn't getting there. I was caught in no-man's-land when Billy Stark headed the ball over my head. I turned round just in time to catch the ball as it bounced back off the crossbar and I'm sure the 40,000 Rangers fans inside Ibrox could feel my enormous sense of relief.

There must only have been seconds left when I threw the ball out to Ian Durrant and he galloped up the pitch before firing a hopeful cross into the box. The next thing I knew McKnight had spilled it and Richard Gough stabbed the ball into the net to make it 2-2. I don't think I've ever celebrated a goal as much as that one and it was the same for all the lads and the supporters. I ran right up to the halfway line to join in and en route I was giving every Celtic player in sight pelters.

'Get that right up ye,' I was shouting to their players, to the Celtic bench and to their fans. I'd completely lost it and I must have created some sort of new world record for getting as many expletives into one sentence as possible. The feeling of sheer ecstasy was magnificent and unless you have ever been involved in an Old Firm match it's almost impossible to convey just what it's like. However, as I was shouting my mouth off and running about like a demented madman, my three false teeth fell out in the centre circle.

I'd lost the teeth in the 1981 FA Cup Final when I collided with my own team-mate Chris Hughton and suddenly, amid all the pandemonium, there I was fumbling about the ground trying to find them. But I had Woodsy's goalkeeper gloves on and they were miles too big for me so when I did eventually locate them I couldn't pick them up. It was a classic comedy moment and in the end I think Derek Ferguson got them for me and stuffed them back into my mouth. Normally I took them out when I played but I was so caught up in the importance of the match beforehand that I simply forgot.

Amidst all the bedlam I'd also forgotten that the game wasn't finished although there could only have been a few seconds remaining. From the kick-off Dave McPherson passed the ball back to me and just after I'd picked it up Andy Walker came flying in and stuck his knee into my thigh. It wasn't that bad a challenge and it didn't hurt, but about ten seconds later I decided to have a delayed reaction in order to waste some time. I had trouble keeping a straight face when the ref came over to see if I was OK. The crowd, who were already going bananas, were loving it and that day was undoubtedly the best atmosphere I've ever experienced. I'm surprised the roof didn't come off the stadium.

The Rangers fans were going through the full repertoire of songs and I was so caught up in the emotion of it all I decided I wanted a piece of this. So I joined in. As I was rolling the ball across the penalty box I started waving my arms and began to conduct the choir. It just so happens the supporters were singing 'The Sash' although, at the time, I genuinely couldn't have told you what song they were singing. My actions helped crank up the decibel levels another notch or two and by this stage the adrenalin was pumping so much I could have flown out of the stadium.

The place was rocking and while I must have been to Ibrox hundreds of times since then, nothing has come close to matching the sheer ferocity of the atmosphere inside the stadium that day. It will live with me for the rest of my life and despite everything that followed I still enjoyed those 90 minutes more than any other game apart from the 1984 UEFA Cup Final win with Spurs.

Within seconds of the final whistle being blown I had gone from the sublime to the ridiculous. I was still screaming at the top of my voice when a policeman grabbed me going up the tunnel and told me I was going to be arrested. I said, 'you're taking the piss mate', told him to get a life and stormed into the dressing room to continue celebrating. But half an hour later, chairman David Holmes came in and told myself, Butch and Woodsy that there had been several complaints about our behaviour and the police had launched an investigation. I half expected Jeremy Beadle to jump out of the showers and tell me it was a wind-up.

Sadly it wasn't and two weeks after one of the greatest games of my life, the three of us were taken to separate cells in Govan Police Station and locked up. McAvennie was taken to another station at the opposite end of the city. During questioning the police claimed my actions were inflammatory and could have started a riot. It was absolute bollocks because there was no fighting after the game, no rioting and no major incidents that warranted our arrest. You can spare me the nonsense that the actions of players can spark crowd trouble. If you can't control the urge to beat the living daylights out of a rival supporter while two teams are trying to win a game of football then you shouldn't be in the stadium. Any punter who resorts to violence before, during or after the 90 minutes should be locked up. Simple as that.

Instead four Old Firm players found themselves charged with breach of the peace because of the weakness of a referee and the ego of a Procurator Fiscal. I'm often asked if I regret my actions, but if I had the chance I would do the same again. All I did was wave my hands in the air and encourage the Rangers fans to sing even louder. So what? I loved playing up to the crowd, I loved playing for Rangers and I loved getting one over on Celtic. They were our biggest rivals and

I couldn't stand them. It was nothing personal against any of their players, but that's just the way I was when I was a professional footballer. I wasn't interested in being anybody's friend and I certainly wasn't going to socialise with the enemy. I didn't like them and they didn't like me. The fact all the Celtic fans hated me just made me more determined and I thrived on that.

The bottom line was I hated losing, especially to Celtic. The Rangers supporters appreciated my win at all costs mentally and that's why I was so popular with them. I didn't do bullshit and I was never one to beat about the bush. I've lost count of the number of times my attitude has worked against me, but that's just me and I don't think I'll ever change.

When I played for Rangers the Old Firm were both sponsored by CR Smith and they would quite often want representatives from both teams to appear at press conferences to help publicise their products. But during my spell at Ibrox I refused to pose for photographs with Celtic players. Why should I stand in some shop, putting on a fake smile and pretending to be the best of mates? That wasn't my style and I would have been a fraud to myself if I'd gone along with that sort of nonsense. Other players quite happily did it and you see Old Firm players endorsing all sorts of products together these days, but it just wasn't for me. There's plenty of time to do that when you hang up your boots. I was in Glasgow to help Rangers win trophies, not to become friends with anybody at Celtic.

I think part of the reason why so many of the recent Old Firm games have been pretty tame affairs is because too many of the players are pals off the pitch. I don't regret not making more of an effort to befriend Celtic players. Life is too short for regrets and I would never change anything that happened at Ibrox that day even if I had to go through the ordeal of another court case and all the negative media coverage.

When I was sitting in the cell at the police station waiting for my lawyer to arrive I was still convinced any charges would be thrown out. Once the questioning got underway the police just kept telling me how my actions could have caused this to happen and could have caused that to happen. If there had been a riot then maybe there would have been a case, but from where I was sitting they didn't have a shred of evidence against me. Petrocelli I'm not, however I knew that waving your arms above your head on a football pitch was not a criminal offence. But a week later we were all informed that the Procurator Fiscal had decided to press charges.

Originally a trial date was set for February before being rescheduled for April. I'm convinced he decided on that course of action because we were three high-profile English footballers. I'm certain if we had been Scottish then the case would have been turfed into the nearest dustbin. Someone wanted to make a name for themselves and at the same time they saw this as a perfect opportunity to bring us down a peg or two.

I still get angry thinking about it even now, although it's Butch and Woodsy who suffered the most as they were convicted and now have criminal records against their names. I escaped with a Not Proven verdict although I'm still baffled by that. In court the prosecution showed a picture of me grabbing McAvennie around the throat, but the Judge said that didn't prove anything. If they had charged me with assault I wouldn't have had a leg to stand on, but the case against me was centred around the notion that I incited the crowd to riot. It was a total farce and it was such a waste of taxpayers' money.

The five months waiting for the trial were a nightmare and I came close to asking for a transfer just to escape the Glasgow goldfish bowl. It was almost too much to handle and I know Terry and Woodsy felt the same way because we had plenty of discussions about it. We felt we were being victimised because of our nationality and heading back to England looked like the best option. I genuinely felt I was being persecuted for absolutely nothing and that was later borne out when I was cleared. If it hadn't been for the tremendous support of the chairman David Holmes, and the manager, then I think we would have packed our bags and headed back across the border.

The chairman was magnificent and proved as good as his word. He promised to stick by us from the minute he walked into the dressing room after that ill-fated match and he did just that. From organising the best lawyers in town to paying all of our legal fees, which must have run into hundreds of thousands of pounds, Holmes and Souness took care of everything.

Amazingly the gaffer even offered to pay for McAvennie's lawyer after I told him the Celtic board weren't prepared to stump up the money to sort him out with a brief. I'd been speaking with Macca and he was worried the case could leave him bankrupt as he didn't fancy having to shell out for his own fees. As soon as I told the gaffer he phoned Macca straight away and offered to get him fixed up with the same legal firm as myself, Terry and Chris. Macca then went back to Celtic and when they still refused to cover his costs he told them he would leak the story of their penny pinching, and of Souness's generosity, to the press. Now that would have been a scoop worth getting hold of.

Celtic were always getting stick for their biscuit tin mentality at the time and a story like that would have been one of the biggest PR disasters in their history. I think they realised that when Macca threatened them and they quickly agreed to pay for everything. Macca called Souness to thank him for his kind offer and the matter was never mentioned again.

The whole time we spent waiting for the trial to take place was mentally draining and it certainly affected my family. I don't think my football suffered as a result because that was the one release I had and the pitch was the only place where I could get rid of my pent-up anger and frustration. My wife was the one who suffered most as the story was constantly in the newspapers and most of the coverage was understandably negative.

The whole matter was blown up out of all proportion and I still can't quite comprehend how a relatively minor incident during an Old Firm match led to 'Goldilocks and the Three Bears' appearing at Glasgow Sherriff Court. Due to McAvennie's flowing locks that's what we became known as in one tabloid paper. That was actually one of the few things that brought a smile to my face during a difficult period. It was five months of hell and in many respects I was glad when the trial actually got underway. I was just desperate for the opportunity to clear my name.

My lawyer was pretty positive throughout and he was confident I would walk out of court at the end of it without a criminal record and with my head held high. I was fairly certain everything would turn out fine although you can never be sure because there are plenty of times when the jury makes the wrong decision. Unfortunately Terry and Woodsy were about to find that out.

The whole experience was pretty surreal and it wasn't until the first morning of the trial when the clerk of the court asked all four of us to stand up and then read out the breach of the peace charges against us that it suddenly became a reality. One by one he called out our names and one by one we replied 'not guilty'. We were all standing there looking at each other and thinking 'what the hell are we doing here?' It was a show trial played out for the benefit of the media and it gave the Procurator Fiscal his fifteen minutes of fame.

The case lasted five days and we would go through the same routine every day. Each morning at 9am I would meet up with Terry and Woodsy at Ibrox and then we would be driven to the court by the club secretary, Campbell Ogilvie. We would then meet up with McAvennie and all of four us would be led to the dock. It was all pretty amicable and every day we would take turns at buying each other lunch in the court canteen. On the Friday when it was McAvennie's shout he bought us all fish!

The trial itself was pretty boring with the prosecution going over and over the events of the game time and time again. My lawyer said there was no point in me going on the witness stand as the prosecution hadn't been able to prove my guilt so it would have been a pointless exercise for me to give evidence.

One part of the trial that really stands out was the evidence given by a policeman who had watched the game from the stand. He claimed that from his position he saw me go over and punch McAvennie with my right hand. They showed him a video of the incident which proved I'd done no such thing. The copper was then forced to admit he was wrong although that just highlighted what we were up against. I'd always thought the police at football grounds were employed to watch the crowd not the match.

On the Friday afternoon we were informed the jury had reached their verdict and as we returned to the dock I felt sick to the pit of my stomach. I'd been confident all the way through the trial that I would be cleared although now I was starting to panic.

McAvennie was the first person asked to stand up. 'Mr McAvennie, the Court finds you not guilty,' announced the clerk.

I thought that was a good omen because it was McAvennie who started the rumpus in the first place and I was convinced that if anybody would get done it would be him.

Then it was my turn. The clerk said: 'Mr Roberts, the court finds you not proven.' I was totally bemused. I didn't realise there was such a thing as a 'not proven' verdict. In English law there's only guilty and not guilty so I was frantically looking around the courtroom for some guidance on what had just happened. Then McAvennie turned to me with that big toothy smile and said: 'Just sit down. They know you did it but just can't prove it.'

I was still in a state of shock when they read out the guilty verdicts on Terry and Woodsy. The colour drained from their faces as their fate was sealed. I've watched the game on video several times since and I still can't believe Terry and Woodsy have criminal records as a result of what happened. The case only lasted a few days, but the fall-out lasted much longer.

This was the ammunition certain sections of the press needed to label me a bigot. For what? Waving my arms in the air and conducting a choir. The Crown never had a case against me and the notion I'm a bigot because of my actions at the end of a highly charged Old Firm game just doesn't hold water in my book. I'm a character and I've always admitted I don't have any time whatsoever for Celtic, but that doesn't make me anti-Catholic. That's why I always have a chuckle when Artur Boruc gets branded a bigot because he winds up the Rangers fans and crosses himself in front of them. Neil Lennon was the same when he played and now he does it from the touchline. I've got no problem with that and good luck to him.

I've already made it clear I don't think an Old Firm game is the time for making religious gestures, but it doesn't constitute a form of sectarianism. Boruc is a character who shows his passion for Celtic whenever he possibly can. That's what football is all about. Yes, he probably oversteps the mark now and then, but you can tell that beating Rangers means everything in the world to him. He doesn't care who he offends and I like that. Football needs more people who can put some colour into the game. I can empathise with him in the fact that I know how it feels to be hated by one half of Glasgow. Like myself I think he enjoys being the villain.

However, like me, he also found himself embroiled in police proceedings due to the Old Firm game being rooted in hatred that stretches beyond football. Following a match at Ibrox during the 2005/06 season, several Rangers supporters complained to police accusing the Celtic keeper of crossing himself in front of the Copland Road. Now I've already stated that I don't think a Glasgow derby is the smartest place for this type of gesture, yet that doesn't mean the Procurator Fiscal should be involved just because a few punters find it offensive. My message to them is: get a life.

Incredibly, it seems that lessons have not been learned from October 17, 1987 when the four of us had to appear at Glasgow Sheriff Court. On this occasion Boruc was spared the ignominy of a trial and issued with a police caution. In effect he was receiving a formal warning as an alternative to prosecution. It is a damning indictment of Scottish football, and the country's society in general, that a religious gesture can be regarded as inflammatory and insulting even if Boruc did do it deliberately to taunt the Rangers fans. The supporters didn't find it offensive when their own players, Shota Arveladze and Lorenzo Amoruso, blessed themselves before matches so why act with such indignation when someone else does it? Only in the west of Scotland could making the sign of a cross or raising your hands above your head provoke such an outcry.

12

OLD SPARRING PARTNERS

If Muhammad Ali and Joe Frazier took part in the best trilogy of bouts in history then there's no reason why I can't slug it out for a third time with Frank McAvennie. We had our fair share of fights on the pitch, we squared up to each other in a courtroom and now we spend our spare time knocking lumps out of each other in the boxing ring. So far there's been a highly disputed draw and an even more controversial decision that went in Macca's favour so it's only fair he gives me the chance to level the series.

Given what happened in the most infamous Old Firm match of all time twenty years ago then a lot of people might have the pair of us down as strange bedfellows. We couldn't stand the sight of each other when we played for West Ham and Spurs and that intense rivalry continued when we were on opposite sides of the Old Firm divide. If it hadn't been for Macca trying to start a fight with the entire Rangers defence at Ibrox back in 1987 then I'm convinced neither of us would have ended up in the dock at Glasgow Sheriff Court along with Chris Woods and Terry Butcher. Yet, if that unforgettable match (sadly for all the wrong reasons) had passed off without incident then I don't think we would have become good mates and sparring partners.

I got to know Macca well during our court ordeal and while we have stayed in touch for the best part of two decades it is only in the past few years that we have become close. In fact we have been appearing together at so many charity functions and golf days recently that we're starting to become like an old married couple. I hadn't seen him for a while when we crossed swords back in 2001 at the first Auld Old Firm match which was held at Ibrox. The game was staged to raise money for the Cash for Kids charity and a whole host of legends from both sides agreed to come out of retirement for the afternoon.

I remember getting sent the itinerary for the day and I couldn't believe the quality of the two line-ups. The Rangers squad comprised myself, Chris Woods, John Brown, Terry Butcher, Tom Forsyth, Ally Dawson, Trevor Steven, Bobby Russell, Ray Wilkins, Robert Prytz, Mark Hateley, Nigel Spackman, Brian Laudrup, Andy Goram, Mark Walters and Neale Cooper. In the Celtic squad were Macca, Pat Bonner, Danny McGrain, Tommy Burns, Peter Grant, Mick McCarthy, Alan McInally, Andy Walker, Brian McClair, Billy Stark, Roy Aitken, Willie McStay, Tosh McKinlay, Owen Archdeacon, Jim McInally and Frank McGarvey.

It was a who's who of Old Firm legends and when the club called me a couple of days before the game I couldn't understand why only 5000 tickets had been sold. The match was taking place during the winter break so there was no other SPL football taking place in the country that day. There must have been some sort of communication mix-up because by the time I'd arrived in Glasgow it was a 50,000 sell-out. Incredibly, a game between a load of old has-beens produced the second largest attendance in Britain that weekend. Only the Premiership clash between Manchester United and Aston Villa at Old Trafford had more spectators.

You can't underestimate the pulling power of the Old Firm and it was never more starkly highlighted for me than that afternoon. The match really captured the imagination of the public so everybody who was involved was desperate to put on a proper show for the supporters. The bookies were even betting on the match and a few of the shrewdies in the Rangers team made quite a killing.

Ally McCoist, who was still playing with Kilmarnock at the time, had backed Rangers at 4-to-1 to win at half-time and full-time. It wasn't looking good when Celtic took an early lead, however in typical Coisty fashion he scored right on the stroke of the half-time whistle to put us 2-1 ahead. It felt just like the old days and the passion and commitment from both sides was incredible.

We ran out 4-1 winners and I felt privileged to be back playing at Ibrox as I didn't think I would get another opportunity when I left the club in 1988. And just for old times' sake I went in goal for the last ten minutes when the game was already in the bag. The whole occasion was an unprecedented success and there were plans to make it an annual event alternating between Ibrox and Celtic Park, but, for some reason, it never materialised.

After that I played in loads of charity games and celebrity tournaments with Macca and, as we both lived down south, we would meet up every now and again for a few beers. Then he approached me and asked if I would be interested in fighting him at a boxing function in Glasgow. The promoter Ian McLeod was organising it and Gordon Smith and the politician Tommy Sheridan were going to be on the same bill at the Marriott Hotel. Just before the fight, Smith had to pull out because he got the chief executive job at the Scottish Football Association and I don't think his new employers were keen for him to box.

Roddy Collins, brother of former Super Middleweight World Champion Steve, stood in as his replacement and gave Sheridan the beating of his life. He battered him to a pulp and after watching the fight I started to wonder what I had let myself in for. I was trying to check out whether Macca's beer belly was bigger than mine to gauge how much training he'd done, but I couldn't see because he had a massive robe on. I'd put in two months of solid training although I'd only done a couple of rounds sparring. I hate losing at anything and I was so determined to win I set up a gym in my garage. I would do as many sit-ups, press-ups, squat thrusts and burpees as possible in half an hour. I'd even bought myself a punch bag so the second half of my session would be spent knocking shit out of that. The Rocky music would be on in the background to get me going and I went through the same routine for eight weeks.

I must have looked a right wally and I'm gutted I didn't make a video diary because it would have been priceless viewing. On the night of the bout there must have been about 500 people at the Marriott so I was just hoping my training would pay off as boxing three two-minute rounds is pretty hard going. It doesn't sound much, but I urge anybody to give at a go because it ain't easy regardless of how fit you are.

While we were waiting to make our ring entrance Macca turned to me and said: 'Just go easy to start with, Robbo. We'll just do a bit of gentle sparring because we don't want to get knackered.' However, less than a second after we touched gloves I caught him a cracker right on the bridge of his nose. He just looked at me and said: 'What the fuck are you doing?' We then went for it hammer and tongs for three rounds and by the end of it neither of us could lift our gloves above our waists.

In the interests of fairness the referee called it a draw and I didn't have the energy to complain. I'm sure there are easier ways to earn £2000 for charity, but I actually enjoyed it and I don't think a pint of lager has ever tasted as good as it did that night.

The re-match was supposed to go ahead in Dubai last year although there were loads of problems with a venue so it was switched to London before getting moved to the Reebok Stadium in Bolton. I hadn't done enough training for the second fight and I don't think it was as well organised as the first one in Glasgow. We were fighting on an amateur bout with proper fighters and I felt like a bit of a fraud to be honest.

Irishman Steve Collins was the referee and before we went into the ring I asked him if this was going to be a draw as well. He said: 'There's no chance of a former Rangers player winning while I'm the referee.' I thought he was only taking the piss although when Macca, who was in even worse shape than me, couldn't lay a glove on me for three rounds and still got the decision I realised he was being serious!

It should all have been a bit of fun but I stormed out of the ring in a right huff because I was so disgusted. Macca had a black eye and was covered in bruises and he even admitted to me afterwards that Collins was just playing funny buggers. I really shouldn't have been annoyed, but I was. It just showed my competitive instinct was still burning strongly and that as I close in on 50 I'm still the world's worst loser.

I've told Macca we have unfinished business to attend to, although given he's 1-0 ahead I don't think he's quite so keen to get back into the ring.

13

SHOWDOWN WITH SOUNESS

The beginning of the end for me at Rangers came in the penultimate league game of the 1987/88 season at home to Aberdeen. Celtic were already champions by that stage but the gaffer was understandably keen to sign off the campaign at Ibrox with a victory and give the fans something to cheer about. As it turned out we didn't just lose the game, I also lost my Rangers career.

Even now, two decades down the line, there is still a great deal of bitterness about the way my time in Glasgow came to an abrupt and unnecessary end. In fact, the more I think about it the more I'm convinced the whole situation was preorchestrated.

The game itself was pretty poor and subconsciously the whole team struggled to lift themselves, knowing our biggest rivals had regained the title we'd snatched off them the previous year. It was a typical, dour, end-of-season encounter that looked sure to end scoreless. Both teams were pretty comfortable at the back but, with about 15 minutes to go, John Brown, my central defensive partner, got injured, and a young Scott Nisbet was thrust into the action.

We'd all been assigned opposition players to pick up at

set-pieces. I was looking after Alex McLeish and Bomber had been keeping tabs on Brian Irvine. Being skipper that day, I told young Nissy not to let Irvine out of his sight if Aberdeen got any free-kicks or corners in the dying minutes of the match. Late on, they won a corner with Irvine stealing a march on Nissie, who was still a teenager at the time, and headed home the winners.

The dressing room was a pretty sombre place after the match as it was a pretty dismal way to finish the campaign in front of our own supporters. But it wasn't long before the silence was shattered. Souness was going berserk, ranting and raving and in those situations it's always best not to make eye contact with him. I was sitting with my head down when I heard him shout, 'it's your fucking fault' at the top of his voice. I looked up at Nissie and told him not to worry about it and to make sure he kept his mouth shut.

'He's not fuckin' looking at me mate, he's looking at you,' Nissy replied, much to my disbelief. Sure enough, I was the one who was getting it both barrels and just to make sure he got his point across, Souness told me in no uncertain terms that I should have picked up Irvine.

'How the fuck can I pick him up if I'm already marking McLeish?' was probably not the smartest response, but that's what I blurted out. 'You're the captain and you should have dealt with it,' retorted an increasingly irate Souness. I didn't really want to drop Nissy in the shit, but there was no point pretending he wasn't responsible. 'I did deal with it. I told Nissy to mark Irvine and if the young kid can't listen then that's not my fault.'

There were all sorts of rumours flying about that I punched

him, but that was total nonsense. Souness did keep going with the verbals before I finally snapped and said: 'That's total bollocks and you know it.'

'Bollocks. You will never kick another ball for this club,' was his parting shot as he stormed out of the dressing room.

Every player in that dressing room knew Aberdeen's goal wasn't my fault, yet not one of them had the guts to stand up for me. Guys like Ray Wilkins, Trevor Francis, Richard Gough and Terry Butcher, who had a broken leg at the time, were all there, but they were all struck dumb. To be honest, I thought the whole thing would quickly blow over as I've been involved in and witnessed hundreds of after-match bust-ups and most of them were a lot worse than my ding-dong with Souness. But the gaffer was stubborn as a mule and he wasn't for backing down.

He told me to stay away from the club until further notice although, as there was only one game of the season left to play – an away trip to Falkirk – I was banking on him cooling down over the summer. I did as I was told and didn't report for training that week, but I decided I'd go to the game at Brockville on the Saturday with Ian Durrant.

The supporters were magnificent that day, singing my name throughout the entire 90 minutes while loads of them had banners saying 'Roberts Must Stay'. Their magnificent backing was much appreciated and it certainly helped boost my ego, but it only served to rile the gaffer who viewed my attendance at the game as insubordination. He phoned me up a couple of days later and told me I was out of order. I was also informed, once again, that I would never pull on the Light Blue jersey ever again. When I was slapped on the transfer list there was a sudden realisation that my 18-month love affair with Rangers was close to being over.

It also made me increasingly suspicious because I knew Souness wanted to bring in Trevor Steven and Gary Stevens and to do that there had to be some departures. It didn't take a rocket scientist to work out who was being sacrificed.

Chelsea were interested but nothing happened over the summer, so I returned to Ibrox for pre-season training only to be told I couldn't take part with the rest of the lads. If I wanted to get a move elsewhere I knew that I needed to be in peak physical condition so I was instructed to train on my own once all the players had gone home.

Every night I would arrive at the stadium just before 7pm and train alone for two and a half hours. It was really weird and I felt like a prisoner inside a deserted Ibrox. It was like being in solitary confinement. I made up my own fitness programme which basically involved running up and down all the staircases inside the ground. Apart from the groundsman and the security guard there was nobody else there and after ten days of putting myself through my paces I decided to contact the Scottish Players Football Association. I'd been speaking to one of my mates and he said: 'What happens if you fall down the stairs and break your leg when there's nobody around to help you?'

The SPFA contacted Rangers and told them that I needed to be supervised by a member of staff when I was training because I could sue them if I had an accident. The upshot of the whole ridiculous saga was that reserve team managers Jimmy Nichol and Peter McCloy had to take turns at staying behind after training to keep an eye on me. To say they weren't best pleased was an understatement. They were at Ibrox all day and then they had to wait until 9.30pm before they went home. They were totally pissed off although it didn't cause any friction between us because they knew it wasn't my fault.

After a second week working on my own I called Souness and asked to see him. I told him that nobody would buy me if I wasn't 100 per cent fit and that it would be in his best interests to let me train with the youth team or the reserves. He agreed. However by the time I'd left Ibrox and driven to Bridge of Allan my wife had received a message from Walter Smith saying I had to keep training by myself.

I've got no idea if Walter was acting under orders from Souness or whether he was the one calling the shots, but I was fuming. Up until the bust-up with Souness I'd been pretty good friends with Walter. We both lived in the same town and we'd quite often go out for a meal or a drink. But, suddenly, everything changed and he became distant. I appreciate that he was placed in an awkward position, but I was extremely disappointed with the way our relationship disintegrated. I expected more of Walter. Still, that's what happens in football and there's no point holding any grudges.

I had no option but to get on with it and while I wasn't allowed to train with the youngsters I was sent with them on a pre-season tour of the Highlands. By this stage I was just desperate to get a few games of football under my belt although I quickly discovered this was yet another punishment exercise. We had arranged matches for Friday and Sunday afternoon so we stayed in Fort William on the Saturday night. Jimmy and Peter were under strict instructions from on high not to play me, so during the first game against Fort William, I just sat on the bench twiddling my thumbs.

As we didn't have a game on the Saturday we were allowed out for a few drinks. All the lads were taking the piss out of me although it was pretty good-natured and we concocted a cunning plan for the following day. A few of them agreed to feign injuries so Peter and Jimmy would have no option but to play me.

I was one of four subs and when three of them were sent on just after the interval the plan swung into action. Or so I thought. One of the boys signaled to the bench indicating he couldn't go on, but as I started getting ready to replace him Jimmy emerged from the changing room with his kit on. It then turned into farce when Peter went on moments later after another one of our players pulled a hamstring. Even if we'd gone down to eight men there was no way I would have been allowed on.

It was pretty pathetic really and I remember it was a huge story in the newspapers at the time. They didn't portray Souness in a very good light although the more they slagged him off the more determined he was to prove a point. And I was the one who was going to suffer.

The following midweek we had another game in Lancaster and it was exactly the same scenario. Under no circumstances was I to get on the pitch. It was pretty soul destroying so I arranged for one of my mates to drive my club car down south as I wanted to get back home after the game as quickly as possible. Souness was in Italy at the time with the first team although he found out I didn't travel back on the coach with the rest of the reserves. Both him and Walter gave it to me both barrels when they came back, telling me I'd shown the club a complete lack of respect. A couple of days before the start of the new season Chelsea came in with a bid of £475,000 and Rangers accepted it.

It broke my heart to walk out of Ibrox for the last time as I'd quickly grown to love the place and wanted to finish my career there, however I knew there was no way I could ride out this storm. Having spent so much time on my own over the previous two months, I'd had plenty time to think about things and I was pretty sure the gaffer had engineered the whole situation.

I could be wrong but this is my take on what happened. I'd just been voted Player of the Year by 40 different supporters' clubs and I was a huge favourite with the fans. Souness knew that, so instead of just putting me up for sale I'm convinced he pre-orchestrated my departure by creating a fall-out after the Aberdeen game. It was common knowledge he was going to bring in Gary Stevens and there's no way he was going to make England's first choice right back sit on the bench. Richard Gough had been playing in that position although he'd always been earmarked to play in central defence. Butch was on his way back from injury so there was a surplus of central defenders with myself and Bomber also at the club.

Souness also wanted Trevor Steven, but he needed cash and I was viewed as a more saleable asset than Bomber. If he'd been honest and just told me he was letting me go as he believed Butch and Gough were a better central defensive pairing then I would have been gutted, but I would have accepted it. Instead we had to go through an unsavoury pantomime and that left a nasty taste in my mouth.

Leaving Glasgow was the saddest moment of my footballing life and it was deeply upsetting that none of my team-mates stuck up for me at the time. Maybe they had been pre-warned by the gaffer to keep their noses out although there were some big personalities at the club at that time and I expected more of them. That really disappointed me and that's why I didn't have any sympathy for Butch when the same thing happened to him a few years down the line.

I have the utmost respect for what Souness achieved at Rangers. He put the club and Scottish football back on the map and Rangers fans have a great deal to thank him for. Almost single-handedly he revolutionised the game north of the border. He left a lasting legacy and if it hadn't been for him then Old Firm fans would never have been able to savour world-class talents like Paul Gascoigne, Brian Laudrup and Henrik Larsson.

Falling out with Souness ate away at me for years and when he was manager of Southampton I telephoned him up and arranged to meet at the team hotel. I was back living in the area at the time and felt it was the perfect opportunity to bury the hatchet. He never went into any specifics about the aftermath of that Aberdeen game although we both agreed to let bygones be bygones. We shook hands and that was the end of the matter.

Now we get on fine. When I was managing in non-league football he was kind enough to bring his Blackburn team down for a couple of friendly matches so there's no animosity on either side any longer.

14

BATTLES WITH BATESY

My protracted move to Chelsea was finally completed just before the start of the new season at the beginning of August. Chelsea had offered £400,000 but Souness wasn't prepared to let me leave for a penny less than £475,000. The two clubs played a summer-long game of brinksmanship before Chelsea chairman Ken Bates finally agreed to meet the asking price.

I'd already met with the manager, Bobby Campbell, and given him my word that I would put pen to paper as soon as Rangers agreed to release me. Everton were also keen to sign me and there was newspaper speculation that Spurs wanted to take me back following the departure of my old friend David Pleat. Much though I loved Spurs I've never been one for going back and, while there was nothing concrete, returning to White Hart Lane was never an option. Everton did want me to join them and they could offer me First Division football which was a massive attraction. However, while Chelsea were only in the Second Division, I was impressed by Campbell and by his ambitions for the club.

My contract had all been sorted apart from a few minor details and in order for the deal to go through I had to meet Ken Bates. I was summoned to his house in Beaconsfield near

Windsor and I can remember driving up a private road to his place thinking this was more impressive than the Castle just a few miles down the road. Part of his estate was a working dairy farm and I recall getting a guided tour and the chance to sample his home-made ice-cream of which he was extremely proud.

Ann, who was eight months pregnant with twins at the time, came along with me and midway through the discussions Batesy turned to me and said: 'Graham, your wife really reminds me of someone, but I just can't put my finger on it.' He couldn't remember so continued talking and we agreed a £1000-a-week deal for me to join Chelsea.

Minutes later he turned to me and said: 'I've got it now. I know who your wife reminds me of. My favourite dairy cow is also pregnant and she looks just like Ann.'

My jaw just hit the floor while Ann got up, stormed out of the room and went back to the car.

I don't know whether he was trying to be funny or if he was just doing what he always does and saying exactly what he was thinking, however it went down like a lead balloon. It was one of the most inappropriate comments I'd ever heard and I just didn't know what to say. There was an uncomfortable silence which lasted maybe 20 seconds, but felt like 20 minutes, and then I left without signing the contract which was still sitting on the table. I spent the next 48 hours in limbo thinking there's no way I could play for someone like that.

However, he later called me up and apologised and claimed it hadn't come out the way he intended. As a result I ended up getting an extra £20,000 signing-on fee although I can't say Ann was too impressed when I did eventually sign after telling her there's no way I would after what happened. Batesy was a really complex character and while one minute he could be the most generous man in the world, the next he was like Scrooge.

The first season we won the league and gained promotion to the First Division and I remember midway through that campaign he arranged a day out at Cheltenham races for us. He hired and paid for a coach and gave us all £1000 spending money. However, there was always a flip side with the chairman. A few months down the line the club held its annual pre-season open day at Stamford Bridge and just before it started, Batesy pulled me into his office. He was surrounded by empty white buckets with 'Save the Bridge' written on them. There had been years of uncertainty over the future of Stamford Bridge, leading to several acrimonious legal disputes about the freehold of the stadium.

'Do you see all those white buckets, Graham?' Batesy said. 'Well, I want you to give them to all the players and collect as much money as possible for "Save the Bridge".'

I said: 'You're having a fucking laugh. We're football players, not fucking beggars.'

'Well, if you don't collect, you don't get paid. It's as simple as that,' he replied.

So off I went with my tail between my legs to tell the other lads the good news.

It's funny now when I think of a Chelsea legend like Kerry Dixon walking round the pitch collecting money in a bucket from the supporters, but it was embarrassing at the time. Can you imagine John Terry and Frank Lampard having to go round at half-time with begging bowls to make sure Roman

Abramovich had enough dosh in his off-shore account to fill their £150,000-a-week pay packets? I earned £52,000-a-year when I was at Chelsea and thought I was reasonably well off, yet *Big Issue* sellers on the King's Road probably take home more than that these days.

Chelsea had just been relegated when I joined them. They went down via the old play-off system, losing to Middlesbrough in a match which was marred by crowd trouble and an attempted pitch invasion. As a result of the hooligans, we had to play our first six home matches of the following season behind closed doors. We got off to a dreadful start although it didn't have any adverse affect in the long run and the club bounced back immediately and emphatically. We were promoted as Second Division champions with 99 points, 17 clear of nearest rivals Manchester City, and scored 99 goals.

The next season Ian Porterfield, who was Bobby Campbell's assistant and first-team coach, left to become manager at Reading leaving a vacancy in the backroom department.

Bobby phoned to tell me the news when I was driving back to Southampton and then said I would need to come back to the training ground as he had something important he wanted to discuss. I was well pissed off because I was only five minutes from my house and it meant having to drive all the way up the motorway to our base near Heathrow airport. When I got back to the ground, he offered me the job of player/assistant manager, but I turned it down because I was enjoying my football and I didn't fancy all the hassle and extra responsibility that went with it. Anyway I was only 31 and felt that was a bit young to head into the coaching side of things.

I knew how difficult Graeme Souness found it to combine

playing and management when I was at Ibrox and I didn't want to alienate myself from the rest of the lads.

But Bobby wouldn't take no for an answer and kept pleading with me to take the job.

Eventually the chairman came in and said he would give me a new three-year deal and exactly the same signing-on fee as when I came down from Scotland.

£100,000 up front was not to be sniffed at so I asked for some time to consider it and talk it over with Ann. Batesy told me I had until first thing the next morning to make up my mind or the offer was off the table. The added security of another few years was a decent incentive, however there's no doubt it was the £100,000 signing-on money that swung it for me. That's the fee Chelsea gave me when I came back down south although I got the impression the deal had certain complications.

As far as I could work out, one of Ken's companies in Jersey bought my house in Bridge of Allan for more than the asking price and then sold it back to another interested party for less. I'm not sure exactly how it all worked out and I didn't ask too many questions because I wasn't too bothered as long as I got my cash.

The one stipulation about my new contract was I had to move nearer to the training ground and Stamford Bridge. I didn't have a problem with that so I took my kids out of their school and nursery in Southampton and enrolled them in a new place in London. I used to drop them off before training and then pick them up in the afternoon as I wanted to get them settled before we moved. We sold our house in Southampton and put all our furniture into storage while we waited for our new place in Farnham to be completed.

We'd just had it all carpeted and put in new blinds and curtains when Batesy went back on our gentleman's agreement.

I'd only bought my new gaff on the understanding I would put down the £100,000 from Chelsea as a deposit. He refused to give me the money and told me he'd lost the paperwork. When I went to see Bobby Campbell he suddenly developed a bout of amnesia and couldn't remember what the original deal was. No matter how many times I went to see him, Batesy still wasn't prepared to cough up. I was livid because I simply couldn't afford to go through with the purchase of the new house. My only option was to take the kids out of their new schools and move back to Southampton. It was a total pain in the arse.

As we'd sold our old house we had to live with Ann's mum and dad for two months until we found somewhere else to live. It was a total cock-up and caused so much hassle because the twins, Sasha and Luke, were not even a year old yet. Eventually we found a new place in Warsash outside Southampton, just a couple of miles from where we'd moved from in the first place.

I'd had enough of Batesy and told him to stick the club up his arse. I was banished to the reserves for my troubles, however I wasn't going to go quietly on this one.

In a final attempt at getting the matter resolved I went to see the chairman and told him I would take the matter to court unless he honoured my new contract. It was to no avail so I enlisted the help of Charles Newman, one of the top and most expensive lawyers in London, to fight my case at the High Court. It transpired that Chelsea had done a similar thing to other players at the club so the English League, the FA and the Players Football Association got involved in the matter as well. In a separate FA hearing at Preston, the club was fined £100,000 for wrongful payments. I was summoned to appear as a witness and when I was at the train station Colin Hutchison, Chelsea's chief executive, and Batesy saw me.

Colin came up to me said: 'The chairman would like you to join him in First Class for the journey.'

I said, 'Thanks but no thanks,' and sat by myself in the cheap seats. I gave evidence against him and the following week they were hammered with a hefty fine – ironically the amount of money they owed me. Chelsea then sold me to West Brom for £220,000 in the hope I would drop my writ against them although I was desperate to see justice done. Batesy had tried to take the piss and I wanted him to pay.

A date was finally set for the hearing although on the steps of the High Court Batesy's legal team offered to strike a deal with my lawyer. The offer was £30,000 cash plus they would pay all my solicitors fees. The cost of my lawyer was almost £50,000 so I decided to accept. It wasn't ideal, but it was better than nothing. I also had the satisfaction of getting one over on him which doesn't happen very often with Batesy.

I was also gutted because I didn't want to leave Chelsea. We had a terrific bunch of lads at Stamford Bridge and my first season there was one of the most enjoyable of my career.

The fans were magnificent but the stadium was a shit-hole. It had a running track around the perimeter of the ground and it really dulled the atmosphere.

Initially I thought I'd made a huge mistake by dropping

down to the second division as we started the campaign off terribly and picked up only nine points in our first eight games. But the team quickly gelled together. We had a really nice bunch of lads and it was like one big happy family.

Like the Rangers nine-in-a-row squad our motto was also 'the team that drinks together wins together.' Most of the boys enjoyed a shandy or two, however while there were plenty nights on the piss there was also a terrific work ethic amongst us.

We were the best team and the biggest club in the league so that made us a prized scalp every time we took to the pitch. We had to be switched on and up for every single game, and we were.

From September through to April we lost only one of 34 games. But, we didn't just win every week, we won in style, playing entertaining football. Our nearest rivals were Manchester City and after they lost 3-2 to Walsall our lead was virtually unassailable.

We had to go to the Bescott Stadium a couple of days later and Walsall were all mouth about how they were going to do the same to us. We beat them 7-0.

Chelsea were so dominant that we won the title by 17 points. Yours truly weighed in with a staggering 13 goals which wasn't a bad contribution for a central defender. That season was the start of the revolution. The club has never been relegated since. The running track has been dug up and cars no longer park on the perimeter of the ground. And since Roman Abramovich ploughed his Russian Roubles into the club Chelsea have become one of the superpowers of Europe. It's an incredible transformation although I bet Phil Scolari doesn't have to put up with some of the shenanigans that went on when Bobby Campbell was in charge.

During my brief spell as assistant boss I remember sitting in Bobby's office one afternoon before a game with Man City when the phone rang. 'I want to speak with Bobby or Batesy and I want to speak with them urgently,' said a snarling voice at the other end. I said: 'It's Graham Roberts here. There's nobody else at the club just now. Can I help?"

'I just want to tell you that Kerry Dixon won't be playing tonight. He owes us £50,000 and he'll never kick another ball for Chelsea if he doesn't pay up immediately,' continued the caller in his menacing tones. I contacted the gaffer, who cursed and swore about a million times before informing Batesy about the situation. Within a couple of hours the matter had been resolved. The chairman had bailed him out. Kerry was a larger than life character, and still is, and he was also a massive gambler. Whether it was cards, horses, dogs or football he used to punt some astronomical sums of money.

Yet, regardless of whether he won or lost a fortune it never affected his football.

He had a blinder against Man City that night, yet only a couple of hours earlier some of the capital's biggest gangsters were threatening to kneecap him. What a legend.

Legend is not a word that springs immediately to mind when I recall another of my former Stamford Bridge colleagues, Graeme Le Saux. Graeme couldn't stand the drinking culture at the club and just didn't fit in. He accused me of bullying him and keeping his complimentary match tickets. That was the responsibility of the captain, although by the time he broke into the side I had been stripped of the armband and placed on the transfer list because of my dispute with the chairman. Peter Nicholas had taken over as skipper by then so he should make sure he gets his facts right. As for bullying, his suggestion is laughable. Yes, the dressing room was a tough, uncompromising place at that time, but any maltreatment was a figment of Graeme's imagination.

I thoroughly enjoyed my short stint at Stamford Bridge and I was sad to leave Chelsea in acrimonious circumstances. It would have been great to see out my career in West London although following my fall-out with the chairman my position at the club had become untenable.

15

FAMILY FALL OUT

They say strength comes from within. Mine came from my mum, Maisie.

When it came to fighting spirit and resilience, Mum wrote the book. She was my soul mate and my inspiration and there's not a day goes past when I don't think of her.

Mum passed away in November 1993 after a gruelling and near miraculous battle against breast cancer.

She was first diagnosed with the disease in 1972 when the doctors gave her just six months to live. But Mum was never one to give up without a fight. And what a fight she put up. She displayed tremendous courage to defy medical opinion for 22 incredible years. Cancer was just a minor inconvenience for Mum and not once did I ever hear her complain about the hand she'd been dealt. Inside, she was going through the most horrendous and agonising ordeal, yet on the outside she handled herself with remarkable dignity.

She didn't bat an eyelid when undergoing various chemotherapy sessions and radiation treatments and, even now, I find it difficult to comprehend what she went through for more than two decades. Mum was brought up during the Second World War and was always going on about the Dunkirk

Spirit. Defeat was never an option for Mum even in a fight when she knew ultimately there could only be one winner.

It is such a difficult experience having to watch someone you love and cherish so much going through such a horrendous ordeal. Yet, until the last two years of her life Mum was amazingly resilient and upbeat. She coped with it much better than Dad and all five children. I tried to pop along and visit her most days and she was always full of optimism and planning for the future. However, in the final 18 months of her life she really began to suffer. A formidable woman became a shell of her previous self and I found it a real struggle to hold myself together when I went back home to see her.

Even then Mum didn't want anybody feeling sorry for her. I just wanted to pick her up and give her a massive hug, but she was far too frail for that. Mum was disappearing in front of me and I felt utterly helpless and useless. We never ever talked about it, however I knew Dad and my brothers and sisters felt exactly the same way.

I completely lost my way when Mum died. I wasn't very good at displaying my emotions so I tried to bottle everything up. In an attempt to run away from my own grief, I immersed myself in work and just shut off completely from everybody else around me.

I was coming home later and later and my marriage was crumbling before my eyes. I had four beautiful children and I hardly saw them. Football was my release from real life I suppose, but looking back, it was a pretty immature approach. We argued all the time and there's no doubt I was much more to blame for the divorce than Ann.

Indeed, while I wallowed in my own self-pity for months

and months she was virtually bringing up four kids on her own. And doing a marvellous job. The reason I struggled to come to terms with Mum's death, despite being aware that it was imminent for quite a long time, was guilt. I was manager at Enfield when she passed away and I'd normally pop in and see her every morning before driving to London later in the afternoon. Mum was still living at home because she refused to go into a hospice. On the day she died I was running late for a board meeting at Enfield and didn't have time to make the relatively short trip from my house in Warsash to Weston. I remember thinking that I would need to take her some fresh flowers when I went round the following day.

But tomorrow never arrived for Mum. I'd been at the ground less than an hour when I got a phone call telling me she was no longer with us. I've always considered myself a strong person both mentally and physically. I've taken plenty knocks throughout my life but I've always been able to pick myself up and get on with it. That's just my nature.

This time it was different and when the finality of the situation began to sink in I just felt every ounce of strength drain from my body.

Instantly I became an emotional wreck and while I'd been trying to prepare for the inevitability of Mum's passing for a while, it just knocked me for six. As well as losing my mum I'd lost my best mate. To be honest I don't think I will ever get over the devastation of seeing Mum pass away at the relatively young age of 62.

Her coffin was taken to the church and I spent the night sitting on the pews outside the room where she lay. I was so wracked with guilt I didn't bother to telephone Ann and let her know what had happened or where I was. In the weeks and months after she was cremated I just wandered around in a daze, oblivious to what was happening around me.

Ultimately, my selfishness led to a parting of the ways with my childhood sweetheart, fourteen years after we were married. There was nobody else involved. We'd just grown apart. I moved out and signed over the house to Ann. All that mattered now was the children, Hollie, Sasha, Luke and Ella. To be honest I've got a lot to thank Ann for because she's brought all four of them up brilliantly and I'm so proud of them.

As with all divorces it became extremely messy when it came down to sorting out our finances. Ann had me over a barrel because she knew I wouldn't do anything that would be to the detriment of the kids. I didn't mind too much as I wanted to make sure they had the best opportunities in life. Ann got the house and virtually all of my money, although I was extremely pissed off when she asked the judge at our divorce hearing if she could get my car as well. I'd just bought myself a brand new Audi convertible with my pension money and she was determined to get her hands on that too. Some women are just never satisfied.

I was completely potless and out of desperation I was forced to sell my medal collection, with the exception of my UEFA Cup gong, and my England caps.

Given that I was homeless and needed a roof over my head, parting with my medals was the only option open to me at the time. Desperate times called for desperate measures.

I'm not normally one for regrets, but this was most definitely one occasion when I would like to turn the clock back. In terms of personal value it is impossible to put a price on mementoes like that. However, through sheer necessity I was forced to get rid of a lifetime of achievements. A lot of blood, sweat and tears had gone into those successes with Rangers, Spurs and England. Now I had to sit back and watch them auctioned off at Sotheby's. They went for £16,000 and I was able to put down a deposit on a new property. I was distraught and at the moment the hammer came down I knew I'd made the wrong decision. I don't even know who bought them, but I would love to one day get them all back.

Throughout her life Mum was the glue that held our family together. When she died everybody seemed to fall apart. We'd never been a really close unit anyway, but there were so many petty squabbles after she passed away and they quickly escalated out of control. Like so many family fall outs, money was at the root of it although I'd been getting increasingly fed up with my brothers and sisters for a while.

I felt Mum was the only one who had really supported me and genuinely wanted me to succeed during my football career. I got the impression the rest of them couldn't care less and were more jealous than proud of my accomplishments. They only ever took any interest when they wanted me to get them tickets or signed shirts. I cannot recall any of my family, apart from Mum, asking how my children were doing. Not once.

My older brother Stephen was the worst and eventually I had just had enough.

Stephen played in a lot of the same teams as me when we were growing up. He was different class as a youngster and he could have made a decent living at the game without any problem. Stephen was twice the player I was, but just tossed it all away.

He wasted a great opportunity. Stephen was one of those people who wanted everything presented to him on a silver platter. He was always taking liberties when I joined Spurs and when we reached the FA Cup Final in 1982 he wanted me to get him 30 tickets for all his mates. Then he wanted me to pay for the lot of them. I didn't mind getting tickets for friends and family, but I certainly wasn't shelling out so the entire street could go to Wembley when I couldn't afford to carpet my own fucking house.

Everything came to a head when Mum was no longer around and I told all four of my siblings I'd be better off without them. That was over five years ago and we haven't spoken since. Unfortunately Dad became embroiled in the feud as well and decided to side with Sharon, Tina, Stephen and Malcolm. I do care deeply about my dad despite losing contact with him. He still keeps in touch with my eldest daughter Hollie and only recently he mentioned a reconciliation. It's time to let bygones be bygones and as a matter of urgency we need to make our peace. He's in his eighties now and I haven't seen him since 2003. I feel ashamed of myself about that.

16

END OF THE ROAD

Leaving Chelsea was a huge relief because, while I didn't want to move on, there was no way I could stomach any more of Batesy. He'd stripped me of the club captaincy and banished me to the reserves after I had the audacity to take him on. Bullies don't like it when you hit back and I'd embarrassed him by washing Chelsea's dirty linen in public.

Brian Talbot threw me a lifeline when he shelled out £220,000 to take me to the Hawthorns and it was ironic that my senior career would reach its conclusion at the club who first tried to buy me from Weymouth more than a decade earlier. I was looking forward to linking up with Brian, a terrific competitor for Arsenal during his playing days and someone who I had a lot of respect for.

Thankfully, the Baggies fans didn't have long memories and they didn't hold the fact I'd turned them down at the 11th hour to sign for Spurs in 1980 against me.

I was fortunate to enjoy great relationships with the supporters at all the clubs I played and it was no different at West Brom. I quickly discovered that fans usually take players to their hearts for three reasons: if you score plenty of goals, if you give 100 per cent every week and sweat blood for the cause or if you wind up your biggest rivals.

In my second game for West Brom we faced Wolves in the Midlands derby. I was marking Steve Bull, who was a Black Country legend and arguably the most famous player in Wolves history.

Bully was a fearsome centre forward and we enjoyed plenty of good battles over the years, but on this particular afternoon he didn't get a look-in. At the final whistle I walked into the centre circle, gestured to my pocket and then pointed to Bully. I don't know why I used to do those things. I just couldn't help myself. The West Brom fans loved it and lapped it up. The Wolves support hated me and within a few weeks of joining a new club I was public enemy number one with our biggest rivals. It was the same at Rangers with Celtic and at Spurs with Arsenal. I should have been in pantomime as I relished being portrayed as the villain.

Some players can't handle stick from opposition fans, but I needed it to produce my best football. The West Brom punters were quickly on side and while we shared a laugh at the end of that derby the smile was quickly wiped off my face a few weeks later.

We suffered one of the biggest shocks in FA Cup history when we not only lost, but were absolutely hammered at home to Woking from the Isthmian League.

It had all looked pretty comfortable for us and there was no inkling of what was to follow when we led 1-0 at half-time. Woking didn't look much cop and there's no doubt we underestimated them after the break. My second-half display was the worst ever. It was amateurish in the extreme and it still makes me cringe when I think about it. Everything happened so quickly and from being 1-0 up we were suddenly 3-1 behind after Tim Buzaglo scored a rapid-fire hat-trick. Having come from non-league football myself I should have been well aware there are a lot of good players at that level. However, I paid a hefty price for not giving Woking enough respect.

Terry Worsfold – the names of their goalscorers are indelibly etched in my mind because they still give me nightmares – made it 4-1 before we grabbed a late consolation.

Woking proved their result against us was no fluke and were unlucky to lose 1-0 against Everton at Goodison Park in the next round. Unfortunately Brian Talbot paid for the debacle with his job and just five games into my West Brom career the club were looking for a new manager. Stuart Pearson took over on a caretaker basis and remained there for the majority of the season. He did a decent job and I recovered sufficiently from the trauma of Tim Buzaglo to be voted Player of the Year by the official West Brom supporters' club.

Just before the end of the campaign, Bobby Gould took over from Stuart and that's where my problems at West Brom began. For no reason I was axed from the team as Bobby changed things around defensively and then I picked up a couple of niggling injuries. At that stage of your career you just want to be playing every week and there's no point sitting on the bench or playing for the reserves when you're 33. Midway through the season I got back in the side. Bobby didn't rate me as a central defender, but he thought I was capable of doing a good job in midfield.

During my stint on the sidelines he told me I could leave on a free transfer if I got myself fixed up with another club.

In the February of 1993, former Rangers chairman David Holmes – who was now at Dundee – called me and asked if I fancied coming back up north. Dundee wanted me to join them as player/manager. It was an offer which interested me so I told David to go through the proper channels and contact West Brom.

The deal should have been a formality although Bobby Gould decided that he wanted £60,000 for me now that I was back in the team and playing. Dundee offered £30,000 and when that was turned down, David contacted me again to say there was no way the club could increase their bid.

The following day we were playing Hartlepool when my studs got caught in a bog of a pitch and I tore the sheaf muscle in my calf. I knew it was a bad one and when I went to the hospital that night I was informed it would be a couple of months at least before I could even start training again. Mentally I was not in good shape because the deal to Dundee had collapsed and now my season at West Brom was over.

I had an operation and two days later I hobbled into training with my plaster cast and crutches. I was walking along the corridor when the gaffer shouted: 'Give Dundee a ring Robbo and tell them you'll take the job. You can have a free transfer now if you want.'

I called him a wanker and threw my sticks at him before falling over and making a complete tit of myself. I did manage to get myself fit before the end of the season although I never kicked another ball for West Brom. My contract was up that summer, although I did think there was a chance of being kept on when Gould was given the bullet for failing to win promotion.

My optimism levels increased when the identity of the new boss was revealed. It was Ossie Ardiles, my former Spurs colleague and a good friend. We had been through a lot together at White Hart Lane and we'd become good mates off the pitch. Ossie regarded me as his chaperone on the park and when I played in midfield I'd always make sure I looked after him. However, all respect I had for Ossie disappeared when he took charge at the Hawthorns. It was not so much the fact he released me, but the manner in which it happened.

As a manager myself, I know difficult decisions have to be made and you cannot allow sentiment to cloud your judgement. On his first day at the club he called me into his office and told me I wasn't going to be part of his plans. There was no 'Sorry, Robbo, but I want to build my own team. Don't take it personally,' or 'No hard feelings, mate, but I'm going to sign some younger guys.' Manners were never his strong suit at the best of times although I was still taken aback by the abruptness of his attitude. He said: 'I'm not giving you a new contract. You won't be figuring in my plans so you'd better start looking for another club.' That was it. He didn't even say hello or thank me for my efforts over the previous two seasons. There was no mention of our seven years in the same team at Spurs. I expected better than that. I deserved better than that.

Positions of power can do strange things to people. I also think it's when you can see their true colours.

17

COURTING MORE CONTROVERSY

At the age of just 33 I found myself on the soccer scrapheap. It seemed like only yesterday I was winning FA Cups and UEFA Cups with Spurs and helping Rangers win the Premier League Championship. Reaching the top of my profession had been a long slog, yet it had passed in a blur. The realisation that it was over was incredibly difficult to accept, particularly because I knew that I would have to enter the real world again. That terrified the life out of me as it meant I would have to seriously think about what I wanted to do for the rest of my life.

I was well rewarded for playing football and was comfortably well off despite playing in an era when the money on offer was peanuts in comparison to the riches at the disposal of players today. Even average performers in the Premiership today can command in excess of £30,000 a week. Good luck to them, because you only need a couple of seasons on that kind of money to set yourself up for life.

I didn't have that luxury when I left West Brom and after failing to find a senior club I got a call from Enfield asking if I fancied going back to non-league football.

I'd completed a pre-season training with Southampton so

I was in good shape. I'd hoped to win a deal at my old stomping ground but I pulled a calf muscle playing in a friendly and they didn't want to know after that.

Enfield chairman, Tony Lazaru, asked me to play a trial match in the Isle of Wight to assess my fitness and after the game they offered me a deal. I got a decent signing-on fee and good wages considering they were only in the Isthmian League. As I'd turned the clock back more than a decade, I decided to go the full hog. I bought my dad's fruit and veg business from my sister Sharon and became a market trader. I made a decent living although I certainly had to earn my money. I used to get up at 3am and on Tuesday and Thursday nights when I trained with Enfield I wouldn't get to bed until well after midnight. I'd thought those days were behind me when I finally got my big break at Spurs, but I had a big mortgage and four mouths to feed so I didn't have much choice.

There's no doubt it was a bit of a come down and some of the customers used to give me some strange looks. A lot of them just assumed all footballers were multi-millionaires, but that wasn't the case back then. On a Friday I was so shattered I needed to go to bed at 6pm so I could get up in the early hours to set up the stall before I went to play for Enfield in the afternoon. Slowly but surely the hours were killing my marriage although I didn't realise it at the time. Since Mum passed away I'd completely immersed myself in work. It was my way of dealing with the situation, but my family life suffered as a result.

Three months into the season a surprise opportunity to go into management arose when Enfield sacked Eddie McCluskey after a run of poor results. The chairman offered me the job so I jumped at the opportunity. I sold the business back to Sharon, at a loss, and became the full-time manager of Enfield. We eventually finished third in the league that season and in my first full year in charge we finished runners-up to Stevenage and reached the semi-final of the FA Trophy.

In the FA Cup we'd progressed through the qualifying rounds to earn ourselves a crack at Cardiff in the competition proper. We travelled over to Wales the day before the game although I was worried about our chances as there was disharmony and an air of suspicion within the squad. For the past few months, money and valuables had been going missing from the changing rooms and it had eroded the trust between a lot of the lads. Just after midnight on the day of the game I was asleep in my hotel room when I got a telephone call from Mark Brewer, a young lad who was part of our squad but hadn't travelled. The previous afternoon Mark had given a few of his team-mates a lift to the stadium where they picked up the coach for the journey to Cardiff.

He was in a right panic when he was on the phone, claiming he knew who the thief was because they'd nicked jewellery and a wallet from his car. I told my assistant, George Borg, and when the players were eating breakfast we quickly checked the room of the player (let's call him Dave) that Mark had pointed the finger of suspicion at.

Sure enough, we discovered jewellery and a large amount of cash. We pulled the player aside and, after initially denying any involvement, he eventually owned up. I didn't want to tell the lads there and then because I knew they would have killed him so, after telling the player to pack his bags and disappear I had quickly to concoct some sort of cover story.

I told them there had been an illness in Dave's family and he needed to get home urgently. George sorted him out with a train ticket and he was just leaving the hotel when his team-mate John Bailey handed him £300. Ironically, John had organised a whip-round so Dave could get a taxi straight back to London instead of hanging about waiting for a train. I took the money straight back off him and when he'd gone I told the lads the truth. As expected they did go ballistic and almost did kill him when he lined up against them for another team later that same season.

I was pretty pleased with my efforts throughout the campaign considering it was my first crack at management although the chairman didn't agree and sacked me when we failed to win promotion. Patience was never Tony's strong suit, but he was the man ploughing money into the club and he was entitled to make whatever decision he saw fit.

The manner of my departure was particularly galling because the chairman had insisted he was happy with the progress the club was making only a couple of days before. I should have known by that stage you couldn't trust anybody in football, but while I wasn't surprised by Tony's behaviour I expected more from my assistant, George Borg. I'd brought him to the club on Tony's recommendation and we gelled well together and got on like a house on fire. Our principles and philosophies were the same and we both wanted to play good, entertaining football. On the day I was binned we had a game at Carshalton and George told me he would take the team that night and then hand in his resignation. However, after the game Tony announced that George had been appointed Enfield's new manager. Stabbed in the back again.

If George had just told me he wanted the job I wouldn't have had a problem. To be honest, I didn't expect him to walk out with me and I would probably have recommended him for the position anyway. But to do things that way was both cowardly and pathetic. What made it even worse was that my mum had passed away a couple of weeks earlier. George knew that yet he still couldn't be straight with me.

Still, I'd also made a decent contribution as a player at Enfield and Stevenage boss Paul Fairclough was impressed enough to offer me a deal. When I signed we had a gentleman's agreement that the club wouldn't stand in my way if a management job came up.

Sure enough, after a couple of months, Yeovil made an approach although the goalposts had now been changed. They wanted me as player/boss, but Stevenage said they wanted £25,000 for me, which was a bit naughty. Paul claimed he never agreed to let me leave for free if I wanted to keep playing and while he was right I thought he was splitting hairs. I really enjoyed playing under him although he changed completely when Yeovil came in and started treating me like a little schoolboy. I didn't need it so I told him to stick his club. They wouldn't release my registration as a player so, for the second half of that season, I temporarily hung up my boots at the age of 36 to concentrate on the coaching side of the game.

I'd only been at Yeovil a week when the draw for the FA Trophy was made and guess who we got in the first round? Stevenage at home. I couldn't believe it. We lost after a replay. Yeovil were bottom of the league when I took over and I couldn't save them from relegation. We drew 4-4 with

Northwich Victoria on the last day of the season when a victory would have been enough to keep us up. In a way it was a blessing that we dropped down a division because staying in the Conference would only have papered over the cracks. They needed a complete overhaul both on and off the pitch as the club was being run into ground. Yeovil were paying players full-time money yet they were only doing part-time hours. I told them if they wanted to stay they would need to train every day and I knew they couldn't do it as they all had jobs. Too many of them had been taking money under false pretences for years and had been allowed to get away with it.

I booted them all out and was only left with three or four guys on the staff. I used all my old contacts in non-league football from ten years ago and proceeded to build a new team from scratch.

There was an incredible transformation the following season and it was good to end on a high when we denied Enfield the chance of promotion. They were battling it out to go up with Hayes, who had a slightly better goal difference. Hayes won their last game 3-0 which meant Enfield had to beat us by four clear goals to pip them to the title.

We only lost 1-0 and I felt so smug afterwards to see George Borg completely dejected. It was a nice moment for me although that wouldn't be the only time I got one over on my former number two.

The following season we were neck and neck with Enfield in the race for promotion back to the Conference. Near the end of the campaign we played them at Huish Park in a potential league decider and I think every man, woman and child from the town was there to support us. There were 8000 people crammed into the stadium and a further 2000 were locked out. There were tractors abandoned all over the place and people were standing on top of combine harvesters so they could see the match from outside the ground. It was like a scene straight out of the Wurzels and it really had to be seen to be believed.

The referee that day was Steve Bennett, who is now one of the top officials in the Premiership, and while I'd love to slag him off he actually had a good game.

We were 2-0 up, but Enfield fought back to earn a 2-2 draw and keep the title race in the melting pot.

Two days later they lost 1-0 at home to Dagenham and that was enough to see us crowned champions. We were presented with the trophy following our last game against Chertsey on the Saturday. I don't know what came over me, but for some strange reason I thought the presentation ceremony would be the perfect moment for a marriage proposal.

I had been going out with Lisa for the previous four years and, every now and then, she would drop subtle hints about me making a proper woman of her. My plan was hatched and after getting the blessing of her parents everything was arranged. The biggest difficulty was actually getting Lisa to turn up at the ground because she worked as a hairdresser and Saturday was her busiest day. Another hurdle to overcome was that she couldn't stand football.

Eventually I persuaded her to phone in sick on the pretence that we were invited to a civic reception after the game. Following the trophy presentation I was making a speech in the centre circle when I asked her to come down and join me.

I presented her with a bouquet of flowers and asked for her hand in marriage. She was absolutely mortified and if looks could kill that would have been the end of me.

There were 6000 people inside Huish Park that afternoon and they were all whooping and hollering. The players, who were standing beside me, were pissing their pants because they could see it was not going to plan. I'd fucked up big style. I just wanted the ground to open and swallow me up but there was no hiding place. She refused to say yes because she was so embarrassed.

Then to make things even worse, the story of my blundering proposal was broadcast on Radio Five Live by Paul Breen-Turner, who was covering the match, and her boss heard it. Lisa did finally calm down although she only agreed to marry me after I'd plied her with a few glasses of champagne. And it wasn't until our big day in Florida 18 months later that she finally forgave me for the most cringeworthy moment of her life.

Winning the League was a remarkable feat and while I would achieve the ultimate high with Clyde when we beat Celtic in the Scottish Cup my stint at Yeovil was hugely satisfying and probably my finest hour as a manager. When I joined them they were £900,000 in debt and teetering on the brink of bankruptcy. By the time I left three and a half years later the debt had been reduced to just £150,000 and the club was back in the Conference where they belonged.

I persuaded Southampton, Liverpool and West Ham to come down to Huish Park for friendly matches and their presence helped put Yeovil back on an even keel financially.

The only negatives about my spell in Somerset were the

travelling and the club's green and white strip. I was still living in London and the seven-hour round trip used to be a killer. I'd sometimes make that journey five times a week, which could be soul destroying. It also almost cost me my life.

One Monday night I got a call from John Fry saying a board meeting had been arranged for the following morning. They always used to hold them first thing because the directors all had other jobs and that was the most convenient time. As I'd left my club car at the ground the previous weekend, my mate Andy Hamilton picked me up at the crack of dawn to take me down to Yeovil. We trained on Tuesday nights so I had to hang about all day before the rest of the lads arrived. Afterwards we were in the social club and they asked me if I wanted a game of pool, but as I'd been up since 4am I just wanted to get back home as it had been a long day and I was knackered. I was on the A303 from Yeovil, which eventually links up with the M3 motorway on the way back to London, and all I can remember is going over the brow of a hill and suddenly being confronted by a deer that was standing in the middle of the road. Instinct just kicks in when you are in that type of situation and my first reaction was to swerve in the hope of avoiding it.

Unfortunately I wasn't quick enough and the side of the car connected with the animal and sent me swerving into the crash barrier at the side of the road.

My little Renault Clio then flipped over and went careering along the middle of the carriageway. It was completely mangled, the roof had caved in and I was lying upside down. I was completely disorientated although I could see oncoming headlights on the opposite side of the road so I deduced that I needed to get out as quickly as possible. Panic set in. I was rigid with fear and desperately trying to get out. Mercifully, adrenalin kicked in and I was able to smash one of the side windows and crawl out. If I had been trapped for another 30 seconds then I would have been a goner. The first passing car managed to brake quickly enough to avoid the debris and then pulled over to see if I was OK. However, just behind it, an articulated lorry couldn't stop. It smashed the back of my upturned motor and knocked it another 50 yards down the road.

There was such a look of relief on the driver's face when he got out of his cab and realised there was nobody in the car when he collided with it.

The impact of the lorry hitting the boot had sent the contents, including my football gear and kit bag, sprawling across the tarmac. I was standing on the hard shoulder shaking like a leaf a couple of minutes later when some of the Yeovil lads who lived in Newbury went past. They were too busy gawping at the accident to notice my holdall lying in the outside lane and promptly ran over the top of it. They suddenly realised it was my wrecked car and after hitting my bag with a thump, the driver, Paul Turner, thought he'd driven over the top of me! I'll never ever forget the look of sheer horror on his face as he ran out of his car shouting: 'I've killed the gaffer, I've fucking killed the gaffer.' Thankfully, I managed to cheat death and all that was lost that night was a pair of boots, some sweaty socks and a kit that I detested anyway. I never did take to Yeovil's strip. It was horrible and as I just couldn't have my team playing in green and white

I changed the away strip to red, blue and white and wore that one as often as possible.

There was never a dull moment and while I thoroughly enjoyed the majority of my spell down there, there were to be serious repercussions for me following a highly charged and emotional Somerset derby. We'd been paired with bitter rivals Taunton in one of the early FA Cup qualifying rounds and the place had been buzzing for weeks in anticipation for the game. Huish Park was not a place for the faint-hearted that day and there was a real edge to the atmosphere as we battled for local pride.

I wasn't playing due to a thigh injury although I would still make a significant contribution from the touchline. The game was scoreless when they were awarded a throw-in just in front of our dugout. As one of their players was running to get the ball I stuck out my heel and sent him sprawling.

I shrugged my shoulders and held up my hands as if to say it was an accident. But Taunton weren't buying it and before I knew it all hell was breaking loose in the technical area. There was a full-scale riot going on and I was right in the middle of it. It was total mayhem as punches and kicks were raining in from all directions. In that kind of situation you can either just stand there and get your lights put out or else you can retaliate. Everybody on our bench opted for the second option and it seemed like an eternity before calm was restored. By that stage players from both sides had become involved and it was a miracle nobody was sent off.

The game ended in a draw so understandably there was a bit of needle in the air for the replay at their place the following week. Taunton were baying for blood and mine in particular.

I thought the safest place to be was on the pitch so I restored myself to the starting line-up. You could feel the tension and I was just waiting for it all to kick off again as the tackles went flying. The crowd went berserk virtually every time one of our players touched the ball and I had the feeling we would do well to get out of this place alive. Our players deserved a lot of credit for keeping their cool and playing some excellent football under the circumstances as we ran out convincing 5-3 winners.

At the final whistle it turned ugly as some of their supporters started pelting us with cans and bottles as we came off the pitch. On this occasion I reckoned discretion would be the better part of valour and bolted into the dressing room as quickly as possible. I was being called every name under the sun as I cowered under a hail of missiles and the players were getting the same treatment. Once they had reached the safety of the dressing room and the brave pills had been taken, they started banging on the windows and responding to the abuse from the Taunton fans. The language was pretty colourful, but I let them get on with it because there was extreme provocation from the baying mob outside.

Two days later I got a call from the chairman saying there had been a complaint from a Taunton fan who claimed I'd sworn at him and threatened him. I did once challenge a Yeovil supporter to a fight when he called me a 'fat useless bastard' and then spat at me when I was coming off the pitch at the end of a game against Reading, but he declined the offer and quickly scarpered. This time, however, there had been no confrontation and I assured the chairman, Brian Moore, that somebody was trying to stitch me up. When Brian told me the police were involved and wanted to speak with me I had a horrible feeling of deja vu. I'd been in this situation before when I was at Ibrox and I couldn't believe it was happening to me again. The police were acting on information received from a Taunton fan and as a result I was charged with the public order offence of threatening behaviour.

To say I was seething is a bit of an understatement. I was incandescent with rage and I just couldn't comprehend how this was being allowed to happen yet again. No matter how many times I pleaded my innocence and explained to the police I was being fitted up they didn't want to know. Six weeks later I was summoned to appear at Taunton Magistrates Court. There was another media circus as the tabloids descended on Devon to see Graham Roberts in the dock yet again. However, the trial quickly descended into farce when the chief prosecution witness failed to appear and the judge decided there was no case to answer. He branded the whole situation a joke and launched a blistering attack on the prosecution for wasting his time. I was delighted to have my name cleared but was furious when it later transpired that the fan had just made the whole thing up to get back at me after what happened in the first match at Yeovil.

To go through that whole process again made me feel sick to the pit of my stomach. I was an emotional wreck in the weeks leading up to the trial and all because some prat thought he could make a name for himself. In non-league football it was a regular occurrence for players and managers to have altercations with the supporters. At Rangers and Spurs I was playing in front of 40,000 every week and there is not the same intimacy with the crowd. In the Rymans League and the Conference there are maybe 2000 people at most games and you can virtually hear every comment from the stands.

As a high-profile ex-professional I used to get slaughtered every time I played and considering I kept going until I was 40, that's quite a lot of abuse.

Ninety nine times out of a hundred it was water off a duck's back as you become immune to criticism. If you did have a bit of banter back then, most of the punters quite enjoyed the interaction as it was something to tell their mates about in the pub after the game. However, there was always the one who would either overstep the mark or else go squealing to the coppers if you told them where to get off. Or in my case didn't say a thing. I just cannot get my head around the fact a fan can tell you to 'go fuck yourself' but if you retort with the same obscenity then you get charged by the police. It's utterly ludicrous and the sooner the police top brass start arresting proper criminals instead of indulging cranks who think it's fair game to start bleating when footballers give them a taste of their own medicine, the better. I'd be willing to bet the fan who made up a complete pack of lies about me was never prosecuted. And what about the copper at the Old Firm trial who said he saw me punch Frank McAvennie? Was he the subject of any internal disciplinary enquiry for making up a complete load of tosh? No, I don't think so, yet I had to be publicly humiliated for months before I got the opportunity to clear my name in court.

I was quite capable of humiliating myself as I proved once again during a match with Heybridge Swifts. We were absolutely awful in the first half and I was reading the riot act at the interval. In the dressing room we had a massive dispenser which held 20 litres of water, but the thing had been empty for the previous three weeks, much to my disgust. I was tearing strips off everybody and was in the process of telling them how they were as much use as the water dispenser when I booted it for added effect.

What I didn't realise was the physio had filled the damn thing up before the match and hadn't told me. As soon as my boot connected the pain went coursing through my body.

I was in so much distress I couldn't continue with my rollicking. My assistant had to continue the team talk as I received treatment on my self-inflicted injury. By this stage the players were rolling about the floor in hysterics. I couldn't blame them.

I was involved in a similar incident when I was in charge at Chesham. Three days before the start of the season we didn't have a goalkeeper when the chairman, Dave Pembrook, called me to say he'd resolved the problem. He'd fixed up Bruce Grobbelaar, although I couldn't understand how he'd managed it as our weekly budget to pay all of the players was £3000. I only had £200 set aside for a keeper. I knew Bruce well and didn't think he'd play for that sort of money, but the chairman said a deal had been agreed and the Liverpool legend would be in goal on Saturday.

After winning our opening two games things started to go a little bit awry in the third. We were 2-0 down and Bruce was dribbling out of his goal and trying to take players on at the halfway line. The crowd loved it even although we were getting hammered. I was furious, not at Bruce, but at the players who had under-performed and were letting them-selves down. I told them so in no uncertain terms and then kicked an ice bucket that was sitting on the floor. It flew straight at Bruce and if hadn't been for his quick reactions then it would have taken his head off. He didn't emerge completely unscathed as the container hit the wall behind him and the ice completely soaked him.

Bruce was sitting there like a drowned rat and I was trying to keep a straight face while attempting to continue my rant. Thankfully, Bruce saw the funny side and while we were a lot better in the second half we still ended up losing 2-1.

Next up, we beat Slough and after the game the chairman gave me a tug. 'We need to get rid of Bruce,' he said. 'We're not going to win the league so there's no point keeping him.' I explained that we'd only played four games and won three of them and that I couldn't axe him as we didn't have another goalkeeper. Dave then proceeded to tell me he'd actually been paying Bruce £700 a week and now didn't think he repre- sented value for money. 'You're the manager and it's your job to tell him his services are no longer required,' he said.

I replied: 'I never agreed to pay him that amount of money and if you want to get shot of him you can do it yourself.' I couldn't be bothered with all the hassle so I resigned after four games of the season. We were third in the league. I'd only taken over Chesham the previous February when they were bottom of Ryman Premier. We won 12 of our last 15 matches to stay up and the outlook looked pretty good after the chairman provided funds to bring in a load of new players during the summer. But, because it was his money, he was always interfering and felt he could have a say in how the team should be run. I couldn't work like that and as I'd had a couple of approaches from other clubs I was confident my record would land me another job quickly enough. A week later and I was the new player/manager of Slough Town.

In February 1998 my spell in charge of Yeovil came to an abrupt end following another clash with my old adversary, Paul Fairclough – yet on this occasion we were not even in direct confrontation. Stevenage had been paired with Newcastle in the FA Cup and I'd asked the Geordies' boss Kenny Dalglish if he fancied playing against us in a friendly to prepare for the fourth round match. Kenny agreed to the game but then called it off when there was a huge media rumpus in the build-up to the game at the Stevenage Stadium.

Stevenage had erected a temporary stand to increase the capacity of their ground and Newcastle had complained because of safety concerns. It kicked off a huge slagging match with the Stevenage players winding up the Premiership big boys at every opportunity and claiming they were running scared. It was all pretty nasty and the *Sun* newspaper, who were sponsoring Stevenage, were loving it as the row provided a host of back-page headlines.

In my opinion all is fair in love and war and if I was in charge of a team playing Newcastle then I would have done everything in my power to get a psychological edge before the game. However, there was a lot of ill-feeling towards Stevenage from the other clubs in the Conference as they felt there was a complete lack of respect. I couldn't resist a dig at Fairclough and the day before the match I asked the secretary at Yeovil to send a message of good luck to Kenny at Newcastle. At the bottom I signed off by saying: 'Hope you beat them because the teams in this division are not all arrogant arseholes like Stevenage.'

You can imagine my horror when one of the Newcastle players slid it under the Stevenage dressing room before the game. It was a Sunday afternoon and I was sitting watching the build-up to the match on Sky Sports when they reported the story about my fax. My plan had backfired spectacularly and to rub salt in my wounds Stevenage earned themselves a replay at St James' Park by holding Newcastle to a 1-1 draw. The following day I got a call from the chairman and I had no choice but to hold up my hands. I was hoping he'd see the funny side of it although I was grasping at straws. Yeovil held an emergency board meeting on the Tuesday night where my fate was sealed. I was out of a job and I only had myself to blame.

From Yeovil I went to Chesham and then ended up in charge at Slough Town. At Slough, Martin Deaner was the chairman at the time and he had grand visions for the club. He planned to build a new state-of-the-art stadium and have Slough in the Football League within three to four years. However, he had loads of problems with the local council about the development of the land and, in the end, I think it just became a logistical nightmare.

Martin was one of the better chairmen I worked under. He let you get on with things while the rest of them all wanted to poke their noses in. I stayed at Slough for 18 months and the highlight was probably reaching the second round of the FA Cup against Macclesfield. We took them to a replay before losing 14-13 on penalties after extra-time. Incredibly it was our regular penalty taker, Brian Hammett, who missed the decisive spot-kick.

Hertford Town was my next port of call after I answered

an SOS from their owner Mike Schulze. Mike was a mate of a mate and I agreed to help out midway through the season. Hertford were in division three of the Ryman's League and they were absolutely awful. Mike had delusions of grandeur and there was no way the club were capable of fulfilling his lofty ambitions. Players kept walking out because they weren't getting paid and some of them only earned £30 a week. The club was a shambles and the scale of the problems hit home to me when the Mercedes I'd been given as part of my package was was repossessed. Our keeper then walked out with eight games of the season remaining over another wage dispute. I had no money to bring anybody else in so there was only one option open to me and that was to play myself.

I was Hertford Town's goalkeeper for the last eight games of the campaign and brought the curtain down on my career against Tilbury at the grand old age of 41. We were 2-0 up with four minutes remaining, but could only draw 2-2 after I threw two into the back of the net. It was the end of an amazing journey that began 25 years earlier at Southampton, yet somehow I didn't feel like celebrating my silver anniversary. Hertford was nothing but hassle and after I got showered and changed I headed off in search of my next challenge.

I found it at Boreham Wood. When I joined them, they were 17 points behind leaders Bedford in the Ryman's First Division with 19 games remaining. We then embarked on an incredible run which saw us win 14 and lose only two of our remaining games to pip Bedford for the title. After helping them win promotion I upped sticks again and headed across London to Carshalton. They were second bottom when I was appointed and at the end of the season we finished seventh.

At the risk of sounding arrogant I was becoming adept at getting teams organised and playing exciting football. I knew exactly what was required at that level, and in my first full season, the club won their only major honour when we were crowned champions.

Our best player that year was a young lad called Byron Glasgow. He was different class at that level although one of my first games in charge summed up what you had to contend with at that level of football. We were playing Oxford City away on the Saturday and the coach was leaving from High Wycombe. We were all set to leave when I realised that Byron wasn't on the coach. I kept ringing his mobile but couldn't get an answer. A few of the lads tried to track him down through his mates although nobody knew where he was. Eventually I got a call from his mum later that night saying he'd been banged up after being arrested by the police on the Friday night.

He was such a talent that I wanted to give him a second chance and when he turned up for training the next week I sat him down and said: 'I'll give you one last opportunity but if you fuck it up you've had it. You can either screw the nut or walk out the door.' He had so many dodgy mates and his attitude did stink at times, but, to his credit, he toed the party line most of the time and if it hadn't been for his outstanding performances every week then we wouldn't have won the league.

Following our promotion to the Ryman Premier I had a fall out with the chairman Steve Friend after going massively over budget during the previous campaign. Despite winning the title he wasn't impressed that it had cost him so much money. Inevitably there was a disagreement when he said the £10,000 overspend would have to come out of my wages. I was on £600 a week and he wanted to reduce it to £250 a week. I said thanks but no thanks and headed off to Spain to set up a kids' soccer school.

I'd had the idea for a while so I decided to take the plunge. There wasn't much to keep me in England. I got some backing from a couple of businessmen friends and I ploughed every last penny of my own money into the venture in Marbella.

It was mainly for the children of ex-pats although there were a lot of Spanish kids who came along as well. The facilities at our La Quinta site were excellent and would have put most of the top clubs in England and Scotland to shame. The feedback I was receiving from the parents was excellent and the business was doing well.

I thoroughly enjoyed working with the kids and while I wasn't making a fortune I was earning a decent living. Through some of the contacts I made in Spain I also managed to bring in extra revenue from sponsorship.

The first twelve months were a roaring success and virtually every age group from Under 7s to Under 14s was fully booked at the start of the second year. However, that's when the problems started. I discovered that trying to get payment from some parents was like getting blood from a stone. They would continually send their kids along without any money and because you didn't want the youngsters to feel embarrassed and miss out you let them take part. The Spanish mums and dads weren't the problem. It was the Brits. Marbella was a haven for gangsters and crooks, who felt they were entitled to get everything for free. Eventually, it became more hassle than it was worth. I didn't need it so I decided to cut my losses and run.

I wasn't sad to see the back of Marbella. The weather was great and it's a nice place to go on holiday for a fortnight, but scratch the surface and you discover a seedier, nastier side. It's such a false place, full of villains trying to get one over on you at every opportunity. Financially, I'd hit rock bottom when I returned from Spain. My dreams of living an idyllic life in the Costa del Sol sunshine had disappeared along with all of my money. I didn't have a pot to piss in. I had no car, no house and no immediate prospect of getting a job. My second marriage to Lisa was already on the rocks and I didn't know where to turn. It's at a time like this when you really discover who your real friends are.

I was still convinced of my abilities as a manager although after being in charge of virtually every non-league team in the south of England I fancied a fresh challenge north of the border. I still had a lot of contacts in Scotland from my spell at Ibrox and was hoping they would come up with something. First I had to find a place to stay and my old mate Andy Hamilton came up trumps. He'd just moved back home after a decade in London and offered me rent-free accommodation at his place in Larkhall. At least I knew I would be safe walking down the street on my own at night. Larkhall has always been traditionally known as a Rangers stronghold and after living there for six months I can assure you it remains a staunch red, white and blue town.

I had only been back in Scotland a couple of weeks when I arranged to meet Andy at a bar in Uddingston called Gariola's. He'd been out for a few jars in the afternoon so I said I would pick him up and take him back to Larkhall. I'd managed to get my hands on a Vauxhall Vectra by this time, but it kept breaking down and was totally unreliable. Shortly after I arrived in the pub a few of the Rangers lads walked in. They didn't have a game that weekend and had been given a few days off. Barry Ferguson, Michael Ball, Allan McGregor, Charlie Adam and Stevie Smith were part of the crowd. When Barry, who used to have a share in the bar with his agent John Viola, spotted me he asked us to join them. I didn't know him that well, but had met him a couple of times before when I was doing hospitality stints at Ibrox and he was always good company. We stayed there until closing time and, while I wasn't drinking, the banter was good.

All the lads were really friendly although McGregor and Ball didn't say too much. They were too engrossed in their game of poker. They did ask me if I wanted to join in, but when I discovered some of the pots were worth over £3000, I politely declined. That was way out of my league. At the time Ball was on £20,000 a week which was more than my PFA pension paid in a year. At the end of the night I gave McGregor and Ball a lift into Glasgow as they couldn't get a taxi and when I dropped them off they left £100 on the passenger seat.

I arranged to meet Barry the following night at the Cricklewood Hotel in Bothwell. I was telling him about my failed business venture in Spain and he said if there was anything he could do for me then he would gladly help out. Andy was taking the piss out of me about the state of my car when Barry put his keys on the table and said: 'Look if your car keeps breaking down you can have mine.' I thought he was pulling my leg, but he was deadly serious. I was now the proud temporary owner of a brand new Honda CRV. It was Barry's club car, although he insisted that he had three others parked on his driveway so I could keep it as long as I liked. I hardly knew him yet he was prepared to bend over backwards to help me out. It was a gesture that was greatly appreciated.

Barry gets a lot of negative publicity, but he has a heart of gold and I'll certainly never forget his kindness.

18

THE X FACTOR GIANTKILLERS

I'd been out of a job for almost eighteen months and beginning to think my days in football were numbered when the opportunity to become Clyde boss arose completely out of the blue. In management, it's always been a case of who you know rather than what you know. And that's what happened with the Clyde job.

I was quite friendly with the chairman of Airdrie, Jim Ballantyne, and I bumped into him at a midweek Rangers match where we were both enjoying hospitality. I'd just been knocked back for the manager's job at Albion Rovers and I was telling him how I was hoping to try my luck in Scotland as there were so few jobs south of the border. He told me he knew a club who were on the lookout for a new boss and that if I could send him my CV he would be in touch. It transpired that Clyde were the club in question because Billy Reid had left at the end of the season to join Hamilton.

Two days later I received a call from their chairman, John Taylor, asking if I could meet him in Glasgow. Clyde outlined their plans for the future and, while it was definitely one of the worst sales pitches in the world as they proceeded to explain how the club had no players and hardly any money for new ones, I was so desperate I would have taken anything that was on offer. Craig Bryson and Eddie Malone were the only two signed players at the club and both of them wanted to leave. It looked a recipe for disaster.

I was told I'd be given a budget of £250,000 to assemble a squad before the start of the new season. That didn't leave too much room for manoeuvre when you take into account wages and signing-on fees although, given that my options were severely limited, there wasn't really a decision to make. I was at a charity dinner at the Hilton Hotel with Andy Goram the following evening when Clyde offered me the job. The package was £25,000 a year plus expenses although within the space of 24 hours my budget had been slashed to £200,000. That just summed up some of the jokers who ran the ship at Broadwood. Given my lack of knowledge about the lower leagues in Scotland I told them my first priority was to get an assistant. They asked me if I had anybody in mind and I recommended Joe Miller.

I'd got to know him quite well on a trip to Dubai when we'd both taken part in a Rangers v Celtic Old Boys game. We'd had a few games of golf together and I knew from our conversations that he was keen to get into the coaching aspect of the game. Joe was very receptive to the idea of becoming player/coach so we shook hands on the deal and he became my first signing. We were under no illusions as to the size of the task facing us and given we only had two players on the books we needed to get to work immediately. I spoke to all my old contacts at Rangers and Joe did the same with all the players he used to share a dressing room with at Celtic and Aberdeen. They recommended plenty of decent players to us, however when I told them the most we could offer was £150 a week they, understandably, didn't want to know.

So with time running out before we were due to report back for pre-season I came up with an idea to put an advertisement in the newspapers saying we were holding public trials. I knew there would be a lot of players who'd just been released by their clubs at the end of the previous season so I was hopeful of getting a decent response. From where I was standing this was the only avenue open to us because if I started ringing around all the clubs, managers and agents it would have taken me months. And time was a commodity we didn't have much of.

The response was overwhelming with over 2000 people calling the club when we placed the advert. It took the office staff a whole week to process them all and then it was my job to sort out the wheat from the chaff. Given we had so many people desperate for a chance to prove themselves, I had to find some criteria to drastically reduce the numbers. Along with Joe I agreed to restrict the trials to players who had played professionally north or south of the border and to those who had non-league experience in England. The final stipulation was they had to be young, preferably under the age of 25. I felt getting a bit of youth in the side was the best formula to go forward. Eventually, we managed to get the numbers down to around 80 and the trials were arranged for the start of June.

It was like the *X Factor* auditions and, to be honest, I felt a bit like Simon Cowell having to tell people their dream of winning a contract was over every few days. If I'd been on the ball we could have made a television programme out of it as, given what happened later in the season, it would have been a huge hit. The trials lasted for ten days and at the end of it we still had 32 players vying for a deal.

The next step was to invite them all back for the start of pre-season training a fortnight later and then start offering the best 20 contracts. Incredibly Clyde didn't even want to pay them any expenses for coming back. These guys had come from all over the country and busted a gut to prove themselves. Clyde then expected them to complete a full pre-season programme without shelling out a single penny until the first game of the season. I told them you couldn't treat people like that and eventually, albeit reluctantly, they agreed to cough up.

The hardest part of the whole thing was releasing the final 12 guys because they had been through so much together. There was one guy who made it through to the last day and I don't think I've seen a better passer of the ball. However, he only had one arm and I had to let him go. That was arguably the hardest decision I ever had to make as a manager. Sadly, you can't have any room for sentiment in that position although I was genuinely gutted for the lad.

What did surprise me about the whole experience was the amount of negative publicity our trials had generated. There were so many people who dismissed it as a publicity-seeking gimmick and in many quarters we were branded a laughing stock. I remember former Partick Thistle manager John Lambie slaughtering us and claiming we would be relegated. There were others who said we wouldn't even get ten points that season so I took great pleasure and satisfaction from proving everybody wrong. I knew we had plenty of ability, energy and skill in the team with guys like Tom Brighton, Eddie Malone and Stephen O'Donnell. It was just a matter of making sure we gelled together as a unit and fulfilled our potential. Considering where we'd come from I think we managed to do that and out of all my managerial jobs, transforming a rag-tag bunch of trialists into a top-class outfit certainly gave me most satisfaction.

Before we knew it, the season was upon us and our first game was against Brechin in the Challenge Cup. We hammered them at Glebe Park, but still lost 3-2 after extra-time.

I got a welcome surprise before the game when I bumped into a Yeovil fan called Jason McGhee. He'd driven the entire length of the country just to wish me well. His gesture was hugely appreciated.

In the league we travelled to Ross County and it was a similar story. We dominated possession, played some great football and got beat 3-1. After I moved Neil McGregor from right-back to sweeper we picked up our first win at Montrose and we never looked back after that. We went on a great run and we started to win most of our games. Long-term inconsistency was always going to be a problem, given we had such an inexperienced side, but we had talent and I had an inkling we just might be able to give a good account of ourselves in the knockout competitions if we got everything right on the day.

In the CIS Cup we were paired with Peterhead after being handed a bye in the first round. The organisers made the draw for the third round before we played our tie so we knew there was a money-spinning glamour tie with Rangers at Ibrox awaiting the winners. I thought if that didn't act as an incentive for my players then nothing ever would. However, the game didn't go to plan as Peterhead took the lead and then Chris Higgins was sent off before half-time. Their attitude was poor and at the interval I went into the dressing room and completely blew my top. I really gave it to them both barrels and told them they would be seeking alternative employment if there was a repeat in the second half.

The response was terrific and we destroyed them with ten men. We won 2-1 although we created enough chances to win half a dozen games after the break. It was the night when my boys became men and I was bursting with pride afterwards. The performance and the opportunity to go to Ibrox as a manager certainly made the long coach trip back down the road a pure pleasure. There have been a lot of highs during my career, but walking through the front doors of Ibrox as Clyde manager ranks up there with the best of them.

The reception that everybody associated with Clyde received from Rangers Football Club that night was simply fantastic. They went out of their way to make us feel special and we almost repaid their hospitality by dumping them out of the cup. Sitting in the dugout watching the boys go through their warm-up all I could think about was what tactics to deploy. My heart told me to stick to my footballing philosophies and throw caution to the wind. My head was telling me to be cautious and to make sure we were not on the receiving end of a real hammering. In the end I let my heart rule my head because the players only really knew one way to play and that was to be positive.

Looking back, I think Alex McLeish, who was the Rangers manager at the time, totally under-estimated us. He thought victory was a foregone conclusion and that's why he made about eight changes from the previous weekend. Unfortunately for Clyde, he decided to put Barry Ferguson on the bench and that's what saved him from total humiliation. I'm 100 per cent certain if Ferguson hadn't been a substitute then we'd have beaten Rangers and there's every chance McLeish would have paid for the loss with his job.

There was no inkling of what was to come when Thomas Buffel scored after four minutes although after weathering an early storm we started to find our feet. We started to pass the ball around and you could see the lads growing in self-belief the longer the match went on. At half-time I was pretty confident and so was one of my best mates, Alistair Donald, who was sitting beside me on the bench. Alistair has done so much for me over the past ten years and I wanted to repay him for a wonderful friendship. He's a huge Rangers fan and I knew it would be a dream come true for him to sit in the Ibrox dugout even if it was with the opposition. Once I'd hatched my plan I had to think of a way to get him on the bench without arousing any suspicion. There's no way in a million years he'd pass for a player so, for one night only, Alistair was the official Clyde doctor.

At half-time in the dressing room he was like a kid in a sweetie shop and along with everyone else I think he sensed that something special might happen. During my team talk I told the players that if we could get an early goal Rangers would start to panic and the fans would get on their back. After I'd given my spiel I was sitting on the toilet when I heard Alistair saying well done to Alex Williams and praising him for his first-half contribution. Alex was always a cocky so and so, but I'll never forget his reply that night. He said: 'We're really up for this and I think we can beat this lot. The gaffer told us we can win it and I believe him.'

After the restart, Craig Bryson quickly equalised to send our small band of supporters delirious. Rangers looked shell-shocked at that point. They were clueless and it wasn't until Ferguson came on with 25 minutes to go that they began to stop giving the ball away. However, the Rangers skipper was powerless to do anything when Alan Lowing brought Robert Harris down in the penalty box and Stephen O'Donnell kept his cool to slot home the spot-kick. There were twelve minutes remaining and I was yelling at the players to make sure they keep it solid at the back. The words were barely out of my mouth when Ferguson sprayed a long cross field ball, our goalkeeper Paul Jarvie came rushing out to cut it out but, instead of booting it out of the park, he reached the end of the penalty box and decided to pick it up. He then realised he was outside the area and in the confusion let the ball run through his legs. Buffel couldn't believe his luck and just tucked it into the empty net.

The players were crestfallen and I instantly knew our chance of causing one of the biggest ever cup upsets had gone. We somehow managed to hold out until the end of 90 minutes although our legs and minds were gone in extra-time. Federico Nieto scored twice in added time and Marvin Andrews was also on target to give the final score a rather lop-sided look. My players couldn't have given any more and they had every right to feel proud of their stunning display, but there's no doubt in my mind that we'd have beaten Rangers if our keeper hadn't fucked up.

To round off a great evening both the Clyde fans and the Rangers supporters were chanting my name at the end of the match. I thought this was as good as it would get. Little did I know that we'd get another crack at the Old Firm just three months later. However, this time there would be no hard-luck story.

The third-round draw for the Scottish Cup is always one of the most exciting moments of the season for the smaller clubs. It provides the minnows with a chance to have a crack at the big boys and there's always the prospect of a massive pay day. The money generated from playing against either of the Old Firm can keep clubs like Clyde in business for years to come.

It was the end of December 2005 and we'd just beaten Ross County in Dingwall when the draw was made. Like every other side from the First, Second, and Third Division we were praying for one of two teams: Rangers or Celtic. I was in the middle of doing a post-match radio interview when I heard this almighty shout. I turned around to see all my players dancing about like maniacs. You didn't have to be a rocket scientist to work out we'd been pulled out against one of the Old Firm. When they told me it was Celtic at home I joined in with the celebrations.

On the journey home there was only one topic of conversation – Clyde v Celtic at Broadwood on January 8, 2006. The players had had a taste of what to expect against Rangers in the CIS Cup and they were desperate to sample the big time once again. I was sitting beside the chairman on the team bus when I told him there might be a possibility of Sky screening the game. I'd done a bit of work for Sky and I knew a few people there who might be able to pull a few strings. By the time we got back to Broadwood, Sky's Jim White had called me back to say there was a good chance of the game being shown live. A few days later it was confirmed, so before a ticket or hospitality package had been sold we were already guaranteed £85,000 from television. That was a massive bonus for the club, although my main priority was figuring out how we were going to beat Celtic.

The result at Ibrox had filled me with confidence and from the moment the draw was made I genuinely did think we had a chance. That's easy to say in hindsight, but while Celtic were a strong, physical team I'd noticed they didn't have much pace and that's the area I planned to exploit. I went to watch them against Hearts and Inverness before we played them although, being the big brave hard man that I am, I didn't go near Parkhead! I didn't think that would be the smartest move so I sent our coach, Dougie Bell, to run the rule over them at home.

As far as I was concerned, Stilian Petrov was the danger man because everything went through him and he was the guy who made them tick. If Petrov played well so did Celtic. All the talk in the build-up to the match was about Roy Keane. He'd just signed from Man United in the transfer window and he was set to make his debut against us. I remember sitting with Joe in my office about a week before the game and telling him how I wasn't worried in the slightest about Keane and Neil Lennon. Keane hadn't played for months after a fall-out with Man United and there was no way he could possibly be match fit. Lennon was a top-class player, who excelled in Europe and in Old Firm encounters, but this wasn't his type of game. Petrov was the only man I was worried about.

The week before the cup clash I went to Tynecastle to have a final look at Gordon Strachan's team. Hearts were leading 1-0 and just as I got up to leave with about ten minutes remaining, Petrov pulled a hamstring. I was absolutely delighted. I couldn't believe my luck. A few Celtic punters spotted me leaving the ground and started giving me pelters, but there was no way they could wipe the smile off my face. Two days before we played them I rang around all my mates and told them to back Clyde. We were 33-1 with some book-makers and I thought that was the bet of the century. Managers and players are not supposed to bet on games they're involved in, but you can always get around minor technicalities like that. This was an offer too good to miss so I made sure one of them placed a small investment for me. Just to give me an added interest!

Celtic had a whole host of injuries at the time and I was convinced the worst we could hope for was a draw. When the team sheets arrived in the dressing room before the game, my optimism levels doubled. Celtic's defence looked excep-tionally vulnerable as Strachan was forced to hand Chinese defender Du Wei his debut and play Ross Wallace, who was a winger, at left-back. Paul Telfer was at right-back and while I liked him at Southampton I knew his best days were behind him. He didn't have any pace and with Celtic playing a 4-4-2, I knew our 3-5-2 system was tailor-made to exploit them down the flanks.

During my pre-match team talk I told our three central midfielders not to be frightened and intimidated by Keane and Lennon. Yes, they were big names who'd achieved so much success in the game, but their legs had gone by this stage. My final words to the players were: 'If you want to make a name for yourselves as footballers then this is the chance you've been waiting for, boys. Don't let it pass you by.'

Yet, while I was confident of causing a major upset and while I had every faith in my players, I was left absolutely flabbergasted by their performance that memorable Sunday afternoon.

Over the past three seasons, Stephen McManus has probably been the best central defender in Scottish football, but that afternoon Tom Brighton took him to the cleaners. If Tom, who has the ability, could produce displays like that every weekend he'd be playing for one of the top teams in the SPL. I'd never seen McManus struggle like he did at Broadwood and I don't think I've seen him toil since. To be fair it didn't help that he had Du Wei alongside him. On a frosty pitch and with the game being played at 100 miles an hour, the Chinese international was all at sea. It was certainly a baptism of fire and if he hadn't been wearing green and white hoops then I could easily have felt sorry for the big guy, who disappeared off the face of the earth after that game and was never heard of again.

He didn't know what day of the week it was as we dished out a footballing lesson to Celtic in front of the nation. The game was arguably the most one-sided I've been involved in. We had three goals disallowed, hit the crossbar, missed a penalty and scored twice. I kept having to pinch myself to make sure this was really happening. When I looked across at the Celtic dugout Gordon Strachan had a look of total exasperation and was constantly holding his head in his hands.

Gordon is a top-class manager and I take my hat off to his achievements at Parkhead because he has done a magnificent job under difficult circumstances. It's hard enough being involved with the Old Firm when the opposition supporters hate you (I should know), but when you get the same level of abuse from sections of your own fans then it must be almost intolerable. Gordon has had to deal with that throughout his spell in charge, yet he has repeatedly confounded his critics by taking the club to new levels in the Champions League.

However, that afternoon in Cumbernauld he didn't have any answers as Clyde destroyed their cloak of invincibility. Twice in the first twenty minutes we had the ball in the back of the net only for referee Kenny Clark to rule them both out. Those setbacks would have killed off lesser teams, but my lads just kept going. We eventually got our reward when Eddie Malone went down the line and whipped in an excellent cross which caught both Artur Boruc and his central defenders in two minds. When the Celtic keeper finally decided to come for the ball it was too late. His misjudgment presented Craig Bryson with the simplest of chances at the back post and he headed home.

I thought our luck had really changed moments later when Du Wei hauled down Tom Brighton in the box and we were awarded a penalty. When the ref pointed to the spot, I was ranting on the touchline with a mixture of delight and fury as I was convinced Du Wei should have been sent off for denying a clear goalscoring opportunity. Still, I expected

Stephen O'Donnell to tuck away the penalty and double our advantage. When Boruc turned his effort round the post it felt like someone had sucked every last ounce of energy from my body. I just couldn't believe what was happening. We'd only played half an hour yet I was already mentally drained.

Mercifully, we only had seconds to wait before goal number two arrived. From the resulting corner O'Donnell swung the ball in and Malone crashed a stunning volley beyond the despairing dive of Boruc.

Inside 45 minutes I'd experienced every emotion known to man and while I was now back on an even keel I was still slightly worried a 2-0 lead wouldn't be enough. It was slightly disappointing we didn't have a bigger cushion because the score should really have been 5-0 at the interval.

It sounds crazy, but that was just the reality of the situation. I knew Celtic would make a few changes at the break and I expected them to come out all guns blazing.

Unsurprisingly Du Wei had been given the hook, but I was quite pleased to see Adam Virgo line up alongside McManus. Mobility wasn't his strong suit and I knew he was low on confidence after struggling to make an impact in Scotland. Sure enough, we continued to get plenty of joy and when Craig Bryson scored a third midway through the second half I knew that was us into the next round. To my horror the linesman then put his flag up for offside and Kenny Clark decided to go along with him. Three weeks later Kenny was in charge of our home game against Airdrie and he came into my office before kick-off.

He said: 'I just want to apologise for almost costing you the match against Celtic.

'I had a look at the game on television when I got home and realised I'd made a mistake with two of the three goals that were ruled out. Du Wei should also have been sent off.

'You really got me out of jail, but don't worry, I'll make it up to you.' Fair play to him for holding his hands up although I don't think I would have been so forgiving if we hadn't beaten Celtic. (Fair play to him also for giving us a penalty as we beat Airdrie.)

Maciej Zurawski scored a late consolation to make it an anxious end to the game.

Those final seven minutes were pure torture and if we hadn't won that would have been the biggest travesty in my career. Thankfully, we held on to spark incredible scenes of celebration at Broadwood. The ground was packed to its 8000 capacity and I'll never forget the look of sheer joy on the faces of our supporters. This was the biggest day in the club's history, a once in a lifetime experience, and it was a privilege to have played a major part. Understandably the players milked it for all it was worth because, for the majority of them, it will be the pinnacle of their careers. They will be able to dine out on the back of this result for the rest of their lives. Reporters will be ringing them up in five, ten, twenty, thirty years time to talk about the day mighty Celtic were humbled.

In the press conference afterwards I could sense there were a lot of disappointed faces because Rangers had been knocked out the previous day by Hibs and now the Scottish Cup was without its other major player. Still, nothing was going to spoil my day and I think lifting the UEFA Cup as Spurs captain is the only thing which comes close to matching our 2-1 win over Celtic.

In the aftermath of the game, Strachan was extremely digni-
fied, which is more than can be said for me. When he came
into my office to offer his congratulations I'd just walked out
of the shower. The only thing covering my modesty was a
towel and I felt like a real prat. The Celtic manager must have
been desperate to get out of Broadwood as quickly as possible,
yet he still took the time to pop in and wish Clyde all the
best for the rest of the season. Once all the mayhem had died
down and the television cameras had been switched off, I
grabbed a glass of champagne and went into my office for a
quiet moment of reflection on the most wonderful and extraordinary day. I'd been there a few minutes when there was a
knock on the door and the chairman, Len McGuire, and Frank
Dunn, a club director, walked in.

'You must be proud of the boys and happy with that result,
Chairman,' I said toasting my glass. To my total astonishment
he replied: 'Not really. It would have been better if they'd
scored as that would have earned us a replay and another
£85,000 from Sky.' I just sat there open-mouthed, unable to
say another word. I'd just helped put the club on the map,
made the biggest news story in Britain and had one of the
best days of my life. Yet here were these two idiots trying to
ruin it. All that mattered to them was money.

The uneasy silence continued for what seemed an eternity
before they eventually got the message and left. I didn't know
it at the time but that brief exchange was to prove the beginning of the end for me at Clyde. In those few seconds I realised
that football didn't matter one iota to these people. On a small
scale it was just a plaything and an ego trip for them.
Everything in the garden had been rosy until that moment.

Sadly things would never be the same again. I'd gone from feeling invincible to feeling as if there had been a death in the family just over an hour after the final whistle. When they walked out I got my champagne glass and smashed it against the wall. I was gutted.

Two of my kids and a load of old friends were up for the game and they couldn't understand why I looked so down in the dumps when I went to meet them upstairs in one of the hospitality boxes. I think they were even more disgusted than me when I told them what had happened. I still feel a lot of bitterness towards a lot of people who ran Clyde at that time and while that incident ensured the day ended on a sour note, knocking Celtic out of the Scottish Cup will always be my greatest achievement in management. Everybody remembers Berwick knocking Rangers out of the same competition in 1967 but I believe this was an even bigger accomplishment. We handed out a footballing lesson to a Celtic team at the height of their powers. We stopped them completing the Treble and fared a lot better against them than Rangers did that season.

With both of the Old Firm teams out of the tournament we harboured serious hopes of actually winning the Scottish Cup. The draw had completely opened up and we genuinely fancied our chances. Unfortunately, our dream died at the very next hurdle when we went out to eventual runners-up Gretna after a replay. Gretna were strong favourites because they'd spent millions buying their way through the divisions. However, we should have beaten them at Broadwood in the first game, which ended scoreless.

Going to Raydale Park was always going to be a tough ask,

and so it proved. The replay, ten days later, was played in the worst conditions I've ever experienced. There had been torrential rain for 24 hours solid and the wind was so strong you could hardly stand up. I'm not making excuses as it was the same for both teams but when our keeper took a goal kick in the second half the ball flew back and went over his crossbar. It was farcical to be quite honest and when Gretna somehow managed to score playing into the wind during the first 45 minutes I knew our number was up.

After the break the wind speed must have been nearing 100 mph and we couldn't get out of our own penalty area. The players couldn't kick the ball more than 20 yards and we did well to keep the final scoreline at 4-0. Gretna thoroughly deserved the win and I said that to their manager Rowan Alexander when I shook his hand at the final whistle. I didn't like him much as I thought he was too full of himself and we'd had a few spats in the past, but his team had played well and I just wished them all the best for the next round.

Of course I didn't mean it as I really wanted them to get stuffed, but I did it out of courtesy. I wish I hadn't bothered as Alexander turned to me and said: 'That was a bit easy, mate. It would have been nice if your team had turned up.' It took every ounce of self-control not to punch his lights out. Comments like that after a match are beyond the pale. It was unnecessary and totally uncalled for although I wish he'd said it in the dressing room when there were no cameras and press men about because I would have decked him. Now I realised why so many managers in our division couldn't stand the sight of him.

Looking back I regret not giving him a good smack. I know

that's no way for anybody to conduct themselves yet it could have saved me a lot of aggravation and heartache. If I'd hit the twat then Clyde would have had no option but to sack me for gross misconduct and that ignominy would have prevented me having to endure the worst period of my life. Sadly I didn't, and from the minute we went out of the cup to Gretna, my rollercoaster journey with Clyde started to go downhill rapidly. I'd scaled the heights but after bringing Clyde unprecedented riches and positive publicity I would soon be plumbing the depths of despair. As a thank you for all my hard work I would be royally shafted, branded a racist and accused of being anti-Jewish.

19

TO HELL AND BACK

The rest of the campaign was a bit of an anti-climax as we struggled to maintain our early-season form. We would eventually finish fifth, which was still an impressive achievement considering we started off the campaign with just two players. I was confident and upbeat about the following season and felt with a couple more signings to bolster our squad, we would make a decent fist at winning the First Division. Unfortunately the final home match when we drew 1-1 with Stranraer would be the last time I ever took charge of Clyde. I haven't worked in football since.

Maybe I should have seen it coming sooner, but I genuinely felt I had a good working relationship with my assistant Joe Miller. Our ideas about how the game should be played were the same, we worked well as a team, and socially I always found him to be good company. There had never been any disagreements until two days after the Celtic game when Joe called me and said he had an idea about how to raise some money for the players and was keen to take them away to Spain for a few days before the next round as a reward for beating his former side.

I didn't think we had enough time to get it all organised

although I was all for having a charity night to raise money for the lads. When I told the chairman I wasn't too happy about going away, I think Joe's nose was put out of joint. Eventually we reached a compromise with Joe and our commercial manager, Jack Rowland, agreeing to organise a charity function at the Thistle Hotel called the Bully Wee Babes Night.

We planned to auction the ball used against Celtic along with the players' boots and the strips they wore while I said I would arrange to get some signed memorabilia from Rangers and Spurs if possible. To be fair to Joe and the staff at the hotel, it turned out to be a smashing night. We showed a re-run of the match, which the punters lapped up, the food was terrific, all the players got engraved silver salvers as a memento and we made around £12,000 from the auction.

A couple of days later I received a phone call from Jack Rowland saying Joe wanted £1200 in cash to pay for the silver salvers and a further £800 to cover the costs of the video screen that was used to show highlights of the game. The screen had already been paid for by one of our sponsors, Colin Carmichael. It cost £150. I told Jack it was nothing to do with me as Joe had sorted out the whole thing, but to make sure he got receipts for everything. Nothing more was said about the matter until a few months down the line when Joe came into my office with another idea for a trip.

This time he wanted to go on an end of season jaunt to Canada. I didn't think the players would be able to afford it but Joe assured me that his mate Derek Noble, who lived out there, would organise the whole thing. He would arrange for us to do a bit of coaching and play a couple of games, but the biggest selling point about the whole trip was that every-body would get well rewarded. The plan was to use some of the money raised from the fundraiser at the Thistle to get us there, pay for all the hotels and the hire of a coach for the week. We put it to the lads and they were all up for it so Joe went ahead and booked it.

Shortly before we went to Canada I bumped into Arthur Numan, who was a good mate of mine. Arthur was the highest bidder at the auction for the match ball used during the Celtic match. He paid £1400 for it, but because he didn't have that much cash on him at the time, he agreed to send a cheque in the post. Jokingly, I asked him when he was going to pay off his debt because the money was going towards the players' pool for Canada. Arthur frowned that David Bowie brow of his and started to shake his head. 'I gave that money to Joe ages ago, mate,' he said.

Unbeknown to me Joe had called him up a couple of days after the dinner and asked Arthur if he could pay in cash. Joe told Arthur the club needed the money urgently so Arthur agreed to meet him at Uddingston train station on a Friday night. He handed him a brown bag with £1400 in it. I never saw any of that money. In fact, to my knowledge the players' pool never actually existed because no bank account was ever opened to lodge the significant funds.

On the final day of the season, twenty-four hours before we left for Toronto, Alistair Donald was my guest at the game with Stranraer. As a thank you for being on the bench at Ibrox he said he would donate £100 to every member of our 18-man squad as spending money for Canada. He was as good as his word and after the match Alistair handed Joe £1800 in cash. We were all in a bit of a rush to make the club's Player of the Year bash that night so Joe said he would give all the boys the money then. He made some pathetic excuse and never turned up.

When we arrived in Canada late the following evening everybody was completely shattered and we all just wanted to jump on the coach and get to bed. But the bus which was supposed to ferry us between different venues didn't turn up, despite assurances from Joe that it would be there. We waited for ages and by this stage it was two in the morning. Finally three people carriers and a pick-up truck turned up, driven by Derek Noble and three of Joe's Canadian mates. The first thing that hit you when they got out of the car was the smell of drink. It was overpowering. I didn't fancy it much but I didn't really have any choice.

When we finally reached the hotel a few of the lads were standing in the foyer looking like they'd seen a ghost. Apparently one of our 'chauffeurs' had driven the wrong way up the one-way system and when she finally started to head in the right direction she was careering all over the carriageway. Not all the lads appeared to be put off by her though and one, who shall remain nameless, spent most of the trip shacked up with her! Some things on football tours never change.

To make matters worse the hotel was a complete shithole. It was right beside a motorway in the middle of an industrial estate. Now, I stay in budget hotels all the time and I'm no snob, but this made the Travelodge look like the Ritz. The temperature was in the nineties every day yet there wasn't even a swimming pool or somewhere where the players could relax. I had bad vibes the minute we arrived in Toronto and they were getting worse with each passing second.

The following day the boys just chilled out in the bar next door and on the Monday we had a coaching session with a group of local kids arranged. Joe and Derek told me we had 250 children booked in, but only 80 turned up. Something strange was going on although I still wasn't sure what it was.

On the Tuesday we had a five-hour trip down to Windsor, which was near Detroit on the American border, for the first game of the tour. The hotel down there was a hundred times better and at least there was a swimming pool this time. We were close to all the bars and restaurants and the boys really enjoyed themselves.

Before the match on the Friday we had two more coaching sessions arranged on the Wednesday and Thursday. They were at separate venues so Joe went to one place and I went to another. This time there were supposed to be 150 kids at each course. Joe had 109 and I had 37. Afterwards I pulled Joe aside and asked him what the fuck was going on. He told me everything was fine and not to worry. He said everything was under control.

During our three days in Windsor, Jeff Hodgkins, the owner of our opponents Border Stars, agreed to provide us with free food as a gesture of goodwill at a smart little place he had called Bar 47, as long as we paid for the drinks. It was a great arrangement and we all made the most of it with everybody making sure they had three courses every night.

On the morning of the game with Windsor Border Stars I asked Joe if there was transport arranged to take the lads to the game. He said everything was in order and the coach would pick us up three hours before kick-off. Looking back it was quite funny but I lost the rag when our coach turned out to be one of those bright yellow school buses. We couldn't fit any of the kit hampers in it and it was a complete disaster, but all the lads seemed to find it quite amusing.

The journey was a joke and the game wasn't much better. There must have been about 3000 people inside the stadium, but the organisation was a complete shambles. Windsor had a running track around the pitch and there were hundreds of kids playing on it while we were doing our warm-up. I thought they would all be gone when the match kicked off but I was wrong. Every couple of seconds another kid would run across in front of the dug out while a few of them were playing on their bikes. I was becoming increasingly frustrated and it didn't help that my players were getting the shit kicked out of them on the pitch.

The Windsor lads were treating it like a cup final which was the last thing Clyde needed after a long and difficult season. I kept shouting at the referee to take control and start giving us some protection. The conversation was a little heated to say the least, but he didn't seem to take on board what I was saying. He just told me to sit down and shut up, which inflamed the situation even more.

The teenagers, who had been buzzing about on their cycles, were now behind me and could see what was going on. They started to wind me up and began to take the piss out of me. Like an idiot I let myself become involved and told one of them I'd let his tyres down. It wasn't said in a malicious way and the lad himself even started laughing. I signed some autographs for the kids, who were Spurs supporters, at the final whistle and posed for some pictures with them.

After the match the school bus didn't turn up to take us

back to the hotel so we had to wait ages for taxis to come and collect us. It was a huge inconvenience given we had loads of kit with us and I was becoming increasingly pissed off with the whole trip. Back at the bar next to our hotel I couldn't find Joe so I went to look for him. Eventually I found him behind a wall with Derek Noble and Jeff Hodgkins, who was counting out a wad of dollars into his hand. When I asked him about it he said it was part of the fee for the game. He claimed we were due $10,000 but had only received half of it. Joe told me the Windsor club secretary would bring the rest of the money to our hotel first thing the following morning as we were due to travel back to Toronto at 8am.

Then next day, surprise, surprise, all the lads were downstairs in the hotel foyer ready to go but, once again, there was no bus. Derek Noble, our glorified but utterly useless holiday rep, piped up and said the coach that brought us down there was too expensive. It cost $1,700, yet apparently the taxi bill was $2,500. Too many things about the tour just didn't add up and I was beginning to feel extremely uncomfortable about the whole situation.

At least when we got back to Toronto we had moved to a much better hotel. It was a Holiday Inn with a swimming pool so we could see out the remaining four days of our stay in more comfortable surroundings. The hotel was at the other side of the city because that's where our second tour game against the CPSL Toronto All Stars was taking place. But Derek Noble insisted we could only stay there for one night because it was too expensive so, after the game, the plan was to head back to the Ritz.

I went to the reception desk and asked how much our bill

was. It was $1,180 for 15 rooms. The other hotel was $1000 so there was hardly any difference. Before we left I had a word and said it would be much better for the lads if we could extend our stay at the Holiday Inn. I asked him how much it was and he told me $1,780. I pretended I'd left something in reception and went back to double check the room rate. The girl on the desk showed me a copy of the receipt for $1,180.

The game itself was another physical encounter played out in the most stifling conditions I've encountered. The heat and humidity were oppressive and some of the challenges were scandalous. Within a minute of the game starting, Neil McGregor was elbowed in the face. He'd just returned to the team after being out for three months with a fractured cheekbone so I started swearing at the referee and urging him to get control of the contest. The tackles were spiraling out of control and at one point I threatened to take my players off the pitch. We ended up winning 1-0 although I was relieved that my none of my players had suffered a serious injury.

On the bus journey back to the hotel, Joe said a few of the players had been asking for some spending money because they were skint. I told him to give them some out of the players' pool. He said he couldn't because it had all gone, so I suggested he take some out of the coaching money we'd earned while we were over there. Incredibly, he claimed that had all disappeared as well. I said: 'Don't wind me up, Joe. There should be thousands still in the kitty.'

When we got back to the hotel I asked him to explain how so much money had just vanished into the air. He just kept repeating that he had used it all to cover the expenses of the trip and not to get on my high horse. By my reckoning there should still have been at least $16,000 in the kitty as we had been paid in cash for the games against Windsor and Toronto and for our coaching sessions. Jeff Hodgkins had also paid for our hotel accommodation in Windsor and that came to $4000. Then there were the funds we raised at the Bully Wee charity night plus the donations made by Arthur Numan and Alistair Donald.

We had a blazing row in the lobby of our hotel in front of the players. I accused Joe of having one over on me and he shouted back: 'What are you saying? Are you calling me a thief? I'm going to have you. I'll make sure you never work in management again, you c***.'

We still had another coaching session do to with the kids on the Monday night and while it was the last thing I wanted to do I knew we couldn't let them down. That didn't seem to bother Joe who went to the pub with Derek Noble.

On the Tuesday the lads wanted to visit Niagara Falls before we flew home on the Wednesday. We had a terrific day although I was shattered when we got back and decided to have an early night. There was a long flight the next day and I didn't want to be in the same room as Joe so I didn't bother going to the bar. I got the feeling that's when Joe, Derek and several players, who should be utterly ashamed of themselves, concocted their spiteful plan to get rid of me.

You could have cut the atmosphere on the flight home with a knife. Joe knew I'd rumbled him and didn't even look once in my direction. Still, it was good of him to fly first class while the rest of us were up the back of the aircraft. On the Friday morning I went into Broadwood to tie up a few loose ends and then headed back down south for a week's holiday before coming back up to Scotland to complete my coaching badges.

I was driving across the border, looking forward to a golfing holiday on the south coast, when I got a call from a journalist asking if I'd split up with Joe. At that stage I hadn't so that's what I told the reporter. The following day reports of a bust-up and a parting of the ways were all over the newspapers. I then got a call from the Clyde chairman, Len McGuire, asking if I could attend a board meeting the following week.

I returned to Glasgow after a quick break and, somewhat ironically, Joe was on the same coaching course at Murray Park. A few of the other lads on the course thought it was quite strange when we didn't say a word to each other, although I tried to play it all down by telling them we'd had a lovers' tiff in Canada.

The meeting on the Monday night was scheduled for 5.30pm and I phoned my secretary Lynne in advance to ask how long it would take as I would be coming straight from Murray Park. She got back to me and said it would take no longer than one hour.

I was sitting in the reception at Broadwood just after five o'clock when the chairman and a couple of other directors walked right past me and went upstairs without saying a word. I was still there at 7.30pm so I asked Lynne if she could find out what was going on as I hadn't even been home to have a shower.

Eventually, directors Frank Dunn and David Boyce and chairman Len McGuire appeared and we went into my office. There were no other board members there, which I thought was strange. I could tell by the look on their faces that something was wrong so I said: 'What's up? Has someone just died?'

The chairman was the first to pipe up, saying: 'Yes there is something wrong, Graham. We've had a complaint about your behaviour in Canada.'

I asked them to elaborate and Len told me the club had received a letter of complaint from Canada alleging I was a racist. 'Is that right? I wonder who that could possibly be from?' I said. 'What do you mean?' enquired the chairman. I said: 'I'll bet you any money the letter is from Derek Noble.' With that their faces just turned white. They asked me how I knew because nobody, apart from them, had seen the letter.

Noble claimed I verbally abused opposition players during the match with Windsor and then made racist and anti-Semitic comments when we played Toronto. He even claimed his 10-year-old son heard me repeatedly calling an opposition player 'Jew boy' and threatening to 'stick him in a gas chamber'. It's bad enough concocting a vindictive pack of lies, but to then involve your own child is beyond the pale.

Clyde later informed me they had received a further three letters of complaint about my conduct during the tour. According to Dennis Hogan and Neil Hanna, another two of Joe's mates, and Julia Doyle, Derek Noble's girlfriend, my behaviour during those two friendly matches was the most disgusting display of racism they'd ever heard. The four letters were almost word for word identical. What a coincidence.

They accused me of calling a black player 'pineapple head', making donkey noises throughout the entire game and then bragging about it in Ye Old Squire pub afterwards. We certainly all went for a meal in that bar together although it was on the

6th of May. It stuck in my head because we were all watching the Kentucky Derby. The game against Toronto took place on the 7th of May so how could there possibly have been a conversation about something that hadn't yet happened?

They also claimed they were standing beside me for the duration of the two games in question. Yet another load of tosh that would eventually expose them as less than credible. Joe threw in his tuppenceworth as well, insisting I had called one of the Toronto players a chimp. For a while he thought he'd got away with it although he too would eventually have his credibility shot to pieces.

I proceeded to tell the Three Stooges – Boyce, Dunn and McGuire – about my reservations concerning the financing of the trip to Canada. The finances for the trip were not handled in a manner you would expect and in my opinion too many of the transactions were not as transparent as they should have been. However, McGuire said: 'I am not interested in what happened with the money in Canada. It's what you said on tour that I am interested in.'

All this would eventually come out at the tribunal and it gave me some peace of mind when it became a matter of public record as it finally proved who was telling the truth.

After that, I walked out of the room and immediately sought some legal advice. I had the impression Joe was trying to fit me up and now everything was falling into place. It was obvious to my mind that Joe wanted my job and the club wanted him to replace me. My lawyer advised me not to say anything else and to keep doing my job so that's what I did. I tied up a few of the boys on new contracts and continued to look for new players to strengthen the squad. A few days later I got a telephone call telling me not to bother coming into the stadium.

Incredibly, I got a subsequent call from the chairman saying, 'I know you've been suspended, but will you keep signing players for us?' I thought: 'What an arsehole – either this man is extremely stupid or more naive than anyone I've ever encountered in a lifetime of football.' I came to the conclusion he was both.

An official letter then followed informing me of my suspension. I was banned from speaking with the players or to the press. I went on holiday for a fortnight and when I returned there was further correspondence from Clyde asking me to attend a disciplinary hearing in Glasgow on June the 21st. In my absence directors Frank Dunn and David Boyce and the chairman had carried out an internal investigation. I'd call it a witch hunt.

I agreed to meet with director John Taylor and Len McGuire, who proceeded to read out a long list of allegations against me. After each one I kept telling them it was all a pack of lies although they didn't seem willing to listen. This went on for over an hour and until they made the first of many slip-ups.

One of the complaints against me was that I had made racist comments against one of the Windsor players in the pub after the match. However, the only time we had been in that bar was the night before the game so there's no way I could have abused someone I didn't even know. At that point they adjourned the meeting. They returned a couple of minutes later and said they would need to make further enquiries.

During the internal investigation, Clyde contacted Stan Adamson of the Canadian FA in an attempt to verify the letters of complaint from Joe's friends. At Clyde's request, Adamson spoke with the match officials, the opposition players, plus the management and coaching staff of the CPSL All Stars. He wrote back to David Boyce informing him he was unable to substantiate any of the allegations that had been made against me. If the claims of the tour organisers were true, then surely one of the Toronto players would have taken exception to my racist and anti-Semitic abuse that supposedly carried on throughout the game?

The only thing Adamson took exception to during the game was my use of the F-word. I hold up my hands to being a bit like Gordon Ramsay when it comes to use of the English language although, in thirty years of being involved in football, I haven't come across a single manager who doesn't swear. And using colourful language does not amount to gross misconduct.

I'd taken along Jimmy Junnor, who was the Clyde kitman and had been on the tour to Canada, as a witness to the disciplinary hearing because contractually I wasn't allowed to have legal representation.

As we were leaving they pulled Jimmy aside and said: 'Please tell Graham to go quietly because we have a very good case against him. Just ask him how much he wants to go.' It was perfectly obvious they wanted me out and I got the impression they were in cahoots with that little weasel Miller.

While I was banned from speaking to the press throughout the whole disciplinary process, Joe was free to blacken my name at every opportunity. It's pretty hard to stomach when you are branded a racist and a Jew-hater in the national media and are being prevented from a right of reply. I knew the truth would eventually come out and that's what kept me going through the darkest days of my life.

The whole process rumbled on through the summer and on the 10th of July I had to appear at another hearing. I made my case and reiterated that every single shred of evidence against me was total fabrication. I also wrote a letter to the chairman pointing out that a blind man could see that certain people at the club were colluding against me and reiterating my concerns about the way large sums of money appeared unaccounted for during the trip to Canada.

After the police were called in, Clyde did conduct an investigation into the cash situation although the fact that they did not take into account anything that happened in Canada seemed bizarre.

The chairman questioned Joe during his investigation, but I got the impression they wanted to sweep everything under the carpet. In his conclusion Len McGuire admitted: 'The standard of bookkeeping was not of a high standard and no bank account had been set up to deal with the funds. Explanations were deemed credible and feasible. No further action will be taken although a reprimand will be given to the individuals involved in the administration of the fund.' It was laughable.

Just before the second hearing, I walked into the office and David Boyce was at the ground. I asked him for a quick word and he said he was too busy as he had a game of golf. I said: 'Excuse me, I couldn't give a fuck if you're playing with Tiger Woods. I want a fucking meeting so get in my office and we can discuss this man to man.'

He was a bit reluctant but eventually he came in. I added:

'You know I'm fucking innocent, but if you want to believe that lying little bastard and his fucking wanker mates and continue with this stitch-up then it will cost you a lot of fucking money. The truth will eventually come out.'

'I haven't got time for this,' he whimpered and then buggered off.

I knew my days were well and truly numbered. They had already made up their minds to fire me so I thought the only way to fight fire was with fire.

Through Jimmy, the board made another approach and offered me a £3000 pay-off. I wasn't interested although I was becoming worried that my Fort William based lawyers were not quite on the ball as I didn't feel they were giving me enough guidance. My reputation, my career and my future were all at stake. This was one battle I couldn't afford to lose.

I expressed my concerns to couple of businessman friends who suggested I get myself sorted with a top-class solicitor as it was going to get even messier. I took their advice and signed up with Harper MacLeod, the best legal firm in Glasgow.

After our first meeting they assured me I had a cast-iron case and that we would take Clyde to the cleaners. Clyde's final offer to me was £10,000 to walk away. Len McGuire called me up at 10.30pm after a board meeting and said I had one hour to either take it or leave it. It was blatantly obvious there was no future for me at Broadwood so told him I would accept £12,000 only on the condition that the club immediately make it public I had been cleared of all charges and that I would leave without a stain on my character.

An hour later they rang back to say the offer had now been

taken off the table. I was found guilty of all charges and sacked for gross misconduct on July the 25th.

At a hearing on the 16th of August my appeal was rejected. To add insult to injury, Joe was appointed as my successor. And didn't he revel in my shame. He couldn't wait to speak to his gullible puppets in the press, who believed every word he told them, and twist the knife just that little bit further. He thought he'd got away with it and pulled the wool over everybody's eyes. How wrong you were, Joseph.

However, I had to go to hell and back before the truth would finally emerge.

The next 12 months leading up to the industrial tribunal were pure purgatory for me and my family. My reputation was in ruins. I was innocent but nobody was prepared to believe me. The year between my sacking and the tribunal was a devastating time.

There were reporters from a Sunday tabloid newspaper camped outside my daughter Hollie's house for days. Every time she stepped out of her home they would ask her how she felt knowing her dad was a racist. It was disgusting behaviour, yet because of the impending legal proceedings we had to suffer in silence.

The newspaper went ahead with the story anyway, making the same false claims as Joe and his Canadian cohorts. All the sources were anonymous, of course, although you didn't have to be Professor Stephen Hawking to work out where the information had come from. However, there was something in the article which would eventually work out in my favour as it claimed they had video evidence of me shouting racist abuse on the Canadian tour.

For a year I was treated like a leper and ostracised from the football world. Nobody wants to touch racists with a bargepole. Throughout that period I had to live with the stigma of being a racist and a Jew-hater. Personally, the anti-Semitic allegations were probably harder to cope with given I'd spent seven memorable years at White Hart Lane. Spurs have always had strong links with the Jewish community and during my spell in North London I built up a large network of Jewish friends. I will be eternally grateful for their support following my dismissal from Clyde, however not all of them were so accommodating. To be honest I don't blame them. If what I was supposed to have said was true then there's no way I deserved their friendship or their understanding. Regardless of how many times I protested my innocence some didn't want to know. That was extremely hard to accept.

I was at my lowest ebb. I felt my life had been destroyed and I just couldn't comprehend why so many people had conspired against me in the cruellest manner possible. I was consumed by rage all the time and the only thought on my mind was revenge. It got to the stage when I could barely cross the front door.

My doctor prescribed me anti-depressants although they didn't help. I felt I was being pushed closer to the abyss. The injustice of the situation was gnawing away at me and making rational thought almost impossible. There were times when I sat alone in my flat thinking what was the point of going on? I considered the various different options – sleeping pills, car hosepipe, a noose. I didn't find any of them appealing.

The feelings of hopelessness lasted for almost six months after losing my job and it didn't help when I was getting abuse from people in the street every time I was in the centre of Glasgow. The Rangers fans were terrific at helping keep my spirits up although when you live in a divided city you have to be prepared for the flip side of the coin. I've always considered myself thick-skinned enough to cope with any verbal assault although this was proving too much to handle.

The lowest and most sinister point came one afternoon when I was driving back to my flat on the waterfront after visiting a friend in Glasgow. I pulled up at a set of traffic lights when this car drew alongside me and someone started banging on my window. I rolled it down and before I could ask what was up one of the two guys said: 'Don't do anything about Miller or you will regret it.'

Joe was always boasting that he had loads of heavy-duty cousins and acquaintances. Maybe this was their way of passing on his regards. I took the threat seriously enough to report it to the police.

I became paranoid and every time I went out I was looking over my shoulder. Eventually, I couldn't take any more and left Glasgow for the sake of my sanity. I moved back down south to be closer to my children. If it hadn't been for their support I shudder to think what I might have done to myself. Glasgow is a terrific city and I will be one of Rangers' biggest supporters until the day I die, but I realise there is a lot more to life than the Old Firm.

I felt much more at ease with myself when I returned to England. I was out of the goldfish bowl and while I still wanted to make Joe Miller pay for ruining my life and my credibility, I decided to channel my aggression in a much more positive manner.

Clearing my name at the forthcoming industrial tribunal became my sole focus as it didn't look like I would ever work in management again. I applied for fourteen jobs including the vacancies at Bradford, Huddersfield, Rotherham and Grimsby after parting company with Clyde, but didn't even come close to the interviewing process. The tribunal would either provide my salvation or be the final nail in my coffin.

My lawyers had been confident throughout the whole process and while I knew we had a cast-iron case I still couldn't fully share their optimism. I'd already been turned over once despite having done nothing wrong so I couldn't take anything for granted. However, my spirits rose immediately after court proceedings got underway and it became apparent that the tribunal chairman, Hugh Murphy, realised Clyde's case against me was a total shambles.

Clyde directors John Taylor and Jim Murray were first up on the witness stand and it was encouraging to see them completely out of their depth. They were utterly clueless and it was a joy to see them squirming in the witness box as my lawyer took them apart.

John's role had been to interview all the players who had gone on tour to gather evidence against me. He claimed five players, four of them anonymous, had signed statements to say I had made inappropriate remarks on the tour. One of them was deposed captain Paul McHale – the same player I'd given a new contract to only a couple of weeks before he was set to become a dad and wanted some added security for his family. I can only hazard a guess at his motives, but whatever they were he should be utterly ashamed of himself. I provided him with the two-year deal he was looking for and this was his way of saying thanks. I don't know how he can look himself in the mirror.

McHale had missed a lot of the previous season after undergoing a hernia operation. He was the club captain, but Joe felt he was a bad influence in the dressing room and suggested we take the armband off him. I actually agreed with him because I thought he was a real shit-stirrer; he had a chip on his shoulder and always wanted to have the last word.

We both decided to make Eddie Malone skipper as he was a headstrong lad and we thought it might settle him down. As soon as we had made the decision Joe proved just what a manipulative little c*** he was by putting his arm around McHale and telling him how I was the bad guy.

When the storm blew up about the Canadian tour, I was informed that McHale went around the dressing room telling the other players not to get involved before signing a statement himself which backed up some of Joe's distorted view of events. I'm sure there were plenty of players in that Clyde team who didn't like me. That's just the way it is in football, but it was very disappointing to find out that he had also made allegations against me which would later be discounted by the tribunal.

The tribunal chairman asked John Taylor and Jim Murray if they had spoken to the 12 other players who were on the tour and they both answered yes. 'Did they back up Mr Roberts' version of events?' he continued.

'Oh yes. The rest of the boys said he didn't do it,' replied Murray.

So from 18 players who went on tour with Clyde, only one was prepared to go along with Joe's allegations. The chickens were coming home to roost and I was loving every minute of it. After what I'd been through I was finally starting to discover my zest for life again.

Mr Murphy, the tribunal chairman, went through Jim Murray like a dose of salts. He said: 'Murray did not give the claimant the opportunity to dispute the allegation and deprived him of the chance to mount a defence against anonymous evidence.'

Basically, it was a stitch-up.

Another round to my lawyer and by this stage Clyde were reeling on the ropes. Thankfully, the judge didn't stop proceedings as I didn't want the punishment to stop. When Len McGuire was asked why he ignored the allegations of missing money in Canada and only interviewed Joe about the alleged financial irregularities at Broadwood and didn't speak to me, he said he didn't think it was worth it. That's coming from a man who was a Justice of the Peace.

Even Mr Murphy admitted it was a total farce. In his findings he said: 'If the allegations against Miller proved to be correct, it is difficult to believe Clyde could have continued to employ Miller. By declining to investigate something that could have resulted in the dismissal of Miller, the respondents [Clyde] showed bias in his favour. Their actions suggested a preference to employ Miller rather than the claimant.'

I got the impression Clyde were scared of opening a can of worms.

The tribunal chairman totally discounted all of the evidence from Clyde and from Derek Noble and Joe's other mates. Their cock and bull story was flawed in every aspect, particularly the part about me boasting of my alleged 'crimes' in the pub after the game in Toronto. We all had a meal in Ye Old Squires bar 24 hours before our final tour match. Julia Doyle and Neil Hanna later tried to retract their statements, claiming they got the dates mixed up but, by this stage, they had already been caught out.

'Virtually all of the evidence the respondents have was flawed in a major way,' Chairman Murphy went on. 'It is either a remarkable coincidence that both Doyle and Hanna mistakenly said that he was there or the inference that Doyle and Hanna, and possibly Noble, colluded is near inescapable.'

The crucial piece of evidence which eventually put the issue beyond any doubt was the DVD of the match against Toronto. When it came to light that Clyde had a recording of the game, the tribunal judge ordered the hearing to be adjourned so it could be presented as evidence. At first Clyde claimed they had lost it – how convenient. But Mr Murphy gave them 24 hours to produce it as this was the simplest way to determine who was telling the truth.

My lawyer arranged to get a copy of the DVD and we spent eight hours going through every second. In terms of clearing my name this was dynamite. The tribunal concluded that a number of the witnesses were not where they said they had been and that, had Clyde watched it, they could not have continued to have confidence in their statements as their credibility had been undermined. Clearly, and now officially, some people were lying through their teeth.

The tribunal also stated that the video evidence showed the fourth official standing near me for the entire match. Had I really been behaving in the way that had been alleged, it's beyond belief that the fourth official would not have taken action there and then.

Witnesses who'd written letters of complaint claimed they were standing within earshot of me when I was supposedly making racist comments. When the tribunal reconvened, we all watched the Toronto match in glorious technicolor although with each passing minute I could see the colour drain from the Clyde solicitor's face. The tribunal panel could clearly see the conspirators were not within seventy yards of me. In fact, they were at the opposite side of the ground selling raffle tickets.

All it showed was me standing with my arms folded on the touchline for the entire match. Apart from shouting and swearing at the referee when my players were fouled, which I had never denied, I spent the rest of the time topping up my suntan in the 95-degree heat.

It had been a long, tortuous journey to find the truth and there were many occasions when I was convinced it would prove to be a fruitless search. I'd been confronted by a barrier of lies, deceit and hostility from so many lowlifes. They had pushed me to the brink and almost succeeded in breaking me. Now I felt vindicated. I'd been cleared and it was finally a matter of public record.

In his summary, the tribunal chairman launched a blistering attack on Clyde Football Club and accused them of orchestrating a witch hunt against me. He explained there was only one person who would possibly gain out of this whole charade. I'd lost my job and the Clyde fans had lost their manager, but, as Mr Murphy correctly pointed out, Joe Miller was the man who had everything to gain. And that's what the whole thing had been about.

It was such a relief to have the ugly stain removed from my character although there was one lingering regret about the tribunal process. Joe had orchestrated the whole thing, but he didn't have the bottle or the balls to see it through to the bitter end. He refused to give evidence because he knew he'd be exposed on the witness stand. Joe thought he was being clever and he was convinced he'd got away with it but the truth came out in the end.

His recent silence has been deafening and I'm wondering whether it was purely a coincidence that Clyde didn't renew his contract as manager following the outcome of the tribunal? In fact, there hasn't exactly been a great stampede of people queuing up to employ him. Given how he chose to conduct himself, I'm not the least bit surprised about that.

Every time I meet a Clyde fan they ask me if I'm still bitter. You better believe I am. I always will be. I was treated like a dog by people who should have known better. Len McGuire was a Justice of the Peace, for goodness' sake. But, in dealing with the allegations against me, I thought he was a weak individual who was controlled like a puppet by the other members of the board.

David Boyce and Frank Dunn led the investigation into the false claims against me and had me hung, drawn and quartered on the basis of five emails from Joe's mates in Canada. There was no 'innocent until proven guilty' with this lot.

When it was all over and I was awarded £32,300 by the tribunal for unfair dismissal, not one person from Clyde had the decency to offer me an apology or admit they got it wrong. I'd been unable to work for over a year because of the allegations that were hanging over me and now I had to foot a £16,000 bill for legal fees. My name had been cleared, but it had come at a substantial cost.

I was broke and unemployed, but at least I was able to walk down the street again with my head held high.

20

LAST CHANCE SALOON

Thankfully, I have been able to move on with my life. I'm now carving out a successful career as an opinionated radio and television pundit with Talksport, Setanta and Sky Sports. I'm still polarising opinion but that's how I've always been. You either love me or hate me. There's never been any middle ground with Graham Roberts.

The media work is fantastic and it's a privilege to get paid for your opinion on a game you care passionately about. It's also great to operate in a stress-free environment knowing the outcome of the match you're covering won't have any direct effect on you.

However, there's still a big part of me that would love to get another crack at proving what I have to offer at the sharp end of football. Football is almost an addiction and the buzz you get from working with players on the training ground and then getting a result on a Saturday is unparalleled. It doesn't matter if you're plying your trade in the Premiership or the Pontins League, the adrenalin rush is still the same.

In management my record speaks for itself. I've been successful with every team I've played for and every team I've ever managed. That's not just a coincidence. As a coach

I've got results and I did it playing attractive football, and on a shoestring budget. But the game has changed so much over the past ten years and it's no longer a case of what you know, it's who you know.

Sadly I can't get a job in the business for love nor money. Indeed, maybe the only thing Joe Miller got right was claiming I wouldn't work in football ever again. Mud sticks and despite being cleared of all charges at the tribunal nobody wants to touch me with a bargepole. I'm almost resigned to the fact that my days as a football manager are over.

It is pretty galling when you see some managers becoming multi-millionaires even when they have a poor track record. Ossie Ardiles has had some disasters as a manager yet clubs still keep employing him. He's made fortunes from football management, and despite failing miserably at Newcastle and Spurs he still landed high-profile jobs in Japan. He then flunked in Israel before getting another job in his native Argentina for less than a year – and still chairmen want to give him a job. There are hundreds of people in the same boat as Ossie and if you're on the gravy train then you're sorted for life.

I was always under the impression that you can con some of the people some of the time but you can't con all of the people all of the time. That doesn't seem to apply to football although you have to say good luck to anyone who can pull it off. But if your face doesn't fit then it doesn't matter how good you are.

I think the reality of my search for a job hit home when even one of my good friends didn't want to touch me because I was perceived as damaged goods. While the racism and anti-Semitism allegations were still hanging over my head,

Airdrie chairman Jim Ballantyne called me up to ask if I would be interested in taking over from Sandy Stewart as manager. He didn't promise me the gig but was more or less saying the job was mine if I wanted it. Less than 48 hours later Kenny Black was appointed the new Airdrie boss and shortly afterwards I got a call from Jim. He said the other directors at the club didn't think it would be a good move because of the negative publicity that had been surrounding me. That is their prerogative and I don't have a problem with that, but what ever happened about being innocent until proven guilty?

The rejections hurt but they haven't dented my self-belief. I still have confidence in my own ability as a manager and I will keep applying for jobs whenever they crop up. Maybe it will never happen, however I still have genuine ambitions to manage at the highest level as I believe I have plenty to offer. I'm a born winner and throwing in the towel has never been in my nature. My phone's always switched on; I'm just waiting for it to ring.